A

TREATISE

ON THE

FAITH

OF THE

FREE-WILL BAPTISTS:

WITH AN

APPENDIX,

CONTAINING A SUMMARY OF THEIR USAGES IN

CHURCH GOVERNMENT.

Written under the directions of their G. Conference

SIXTH EDITION.

DOVER:

PUBLISHED BY THE FREE-WILL BAPTIST PRINTING ESTABLISHMENT.

William Burr.....Printer.

1854.

ADVERTISEMENT.

REPEATED requests having been made for the publication of our views on Scripture doctrine, the subject was taken up by the General Conference in 1832, and, after carefully considering the pressing calls for such a work, and offering prayer to God for direction, the following conclusion was made:

"Agreed, that the exigency of the times renders it necessary that we publish a Treatise, embracing all the leading points of the doctrine and practice of the Free-will Baptists, giving our scriptural reasons therefor, also our reasons for taking the Holy Scriptures as our only rule of faith and practice."

A committee was then appointed to write a Treatise, and directions were given that the Publishing Committee examine the work when written, and present it to the next General Conference, with their report on the same. Accordingly a draft was made and presented, though not sufficiently prepared for the press. Whereupon, the following measure was taken:

"Agreed, 1. That this Conference, having heard the Treatise read several times, and having carefully considered it, approve of the sentiments therein contained, in connection with certain amendments, and that we now commit the Treatise and the amendments to the Publishing Committee and Book Agent, with instructions to revise and abridge the same, as they may think proper, without changing the sentiments. 2. That a committee of five be raised, whose duty it shall be, when notified by the Publishing Committee, to sit with them and examine the work, give it another revision, if necessary, and certify that the sentiments contained in the Treatise and amendments have been retained by the Publishing Committee. 3. That Elders John Buzzell, Henry Hobbs, Enoch Place, Joseph White, and Hosea Quinby be the above committee."

This certifies, that we have attended to the duty assigned us by the General Conference in revising the following work. We regret that our ability and circumstances have not permitted us to bestow upon it the labor that the importance of the subject demands. A more critical revision would increase its value; but as we are unable to bestow further attention to it we submit it for publication; earnestly praying that our Heavenly Father will be pleased to make it a blessing to our churches, and to thousands who are inquiring after truth.

SAMUEL B. DYER,		*Publishing*
ARTHUR CAVERNO,*		*Committee*
SILAS CURTIS,	}	*chosen by the*
WM. BURR,		*Gen. Conference*
DANIEL P. CILLEY,		*in* 1833.
DAVID MARKS,		*Book Agent.*

Dover, N. H., April 23, 1834.

This certifies that we have examined the following Treatise, as revised by the Publishing Committee, carefully compared it with the original manuscript, and given it what further revision our ability and circumstances would admit. The sentiments, read and approved by the General Conference, have been, in our opinion, scrupulously retained in the revision.

JOHN BUZZELL,		*Committee chosen*
HENRY HOBBS,		*by Gen. Conference*
ENOCH PLACE,	}	*to examine the*
JOSEPH WHITE,		*revised MS. of the*
HOSEA QUINBY,		*following work.*

Dover, N. H., April 23, 1834.

* Since the above Committee was chosen, brother SAMUEL BEEDE has deceased, and Eld. A. CAVERNO has been elected to fill the vacancy. See the Minutes of the 7th General Conference—page 14.

INTRODUCTION.

1. Rise of the Free-will Baptists. In the year 1770, Benjamin Randall, who, under God, was the founder of the Free-will Baptist denomination, was converted through the instrumentality of George Whitefield. In 1776, he was baptized by Eld. Wm. Hooper, of Madbury, and united with the Baptist denomination. At this time divisions respecting doctrine were little known among the Baptists in New England. Randall, however, held to general sentiments; nor was he at first aware that he differed from his brethren, as discussions upon this subject were not then frequent. He felt a serious conviction of duty to come forward as a preacher of the gospel, and soon after commenced his public labors. Shortly after this, a difference of sentiment was perceived among the preachers, and Randall was publicly called to an account, because he did not preach Calvinian election, but *free salvation*. As the brethren came to ex-

amine these points, a division was manifest; for some found themselves in fellowship with the doctrine of unconditional election and reprobation, while others thought it erroneous. Hence, they took different positions, according to their views. Randall joined a church in Barrington that held general sentiments; and, in 1780, was ordained an evangelist. In the same year he gathered a church in New Durham, New Hampshire. As Randall held to the freedom of the will, and that all men may be regenerated in this life and fitted for heaven, through improving the means of grace which God has bestowed upon them, he and his adherents were by their opponents, reproachfully called *Freewillers*. Hence this church received the distinctive title, *Free-will Baptist*. They took the Bible as their only rule of faith and practice; and Elder Randall was selected to write a summary of the doctrine contained in the Scriptures. Accordingly, he wrote thirteen articles and a covenant, which the members of the church all signed. These articles, however, were afterwards laid aside. The church held a conference once a month, which was called a *monthly meeting*. As their number increased, it was soon found impracticable for all to meet at one place, and other monthly meetings were established. They also held a general meeting once in three months, which was called a *quarterly meeting*. The vine shortly extended to other towns and states, and other quarterly meetings were held. At length, yearly meetings were organized by a delegation from the quarterly meetings; and in 1827 the General Conference was instituted by a delegation from the several yearly meetings. In this Conference, twenty-five yearly meetings are associated. There are now [1854] in connexion, 129 quarterly meetings, comprising 1146 churches, 916 ordained preachers, 153 licentiates, and 49,274 members.

2. THE SCRIPTURES OUR ONLY RULE OF FAITH AND PRACTICE. The Holy Scriptures are the writings of the Old and New Testaments.† The apostle says, 2 Tim. 3: 16, 17, "All Scripture is given by inspiration of God;—that the man of

† It should not be understood, that all those whose words are recorded in Scripture were divinely inspired; for the Bible contains the words of wicked men and devils; but that the authors of the sacred books were inspired to write what they have recorded, all of which is designed for our instruction. That the Scriptures are authentic and given by inspiration, may be clearly prov-

God may be perfect, thoroughly furnished unto all good works." Consequently, the

---

ed, independently from their own testimony. The following arguments respect the New Testament, and these, or similar ones, might also be applied to the Old Testament.

1. *The Scriptures were written at the age they purport.* Their style bears the impress of that age. Shortly after the time in which they purport to have been written, they were collected, translated into different languages, and read in different countries. They have been quoted, or referred to, by a connected series of writers, both infidel and Christian, beginning with the cotemporaries of the reputed authors, and extending to the present day. No Scripture, purporting to be the New Testament, and to have been written at any other time, has been quoted or referred to by any other writer. Therefore, the evidence is clear, that the books of the New Testament were written neither anterior nor posterior to the time they pretend to have been written.

2. *The books of the New Testament were written by the authors whose names they bear.* They cannot be the production of one man, as they are so different in style and give relations of the same facts with such slight variations, (not contradictions,) as might be expected from different beholders, giving their relation separately, at different times, and under various circumstances.—The cotemporaries of the apostles, whose writings are now extant, and the early writers, both Christian and infidel, ascribe these Scriptures to the authors whose names they bear. If they are not authentic, some others of the same age and existing under similar circumstances, must have been their authors. But it is much less credible that any other persons wrote the Scriptures, than those who are reputed to have written them; and even if they had, the imposition would have been exposed, and those to whom they were sent

Scriptures have the highest authority over man, so far as they reveal the will of God

---

would have rejected them, especially as their reception was the source of great trouble.

3. *Those authors were virtuous men and gave a true account.* Had they been vicious men, they could not, at this corrupt age, have conceived of so high a standard of morality; and, even if they could, it is incredible to suppose that they would have intruded upon their own criminal indulgences, by publishing it to the world. A wicked man would not be likely to publish a lie, which he could not expect to advance his interest, ease, or reputation. But instead of having the prospect of this, those who came out so much at variance with the prevailing customs of the times, as did the authors of the Scriptures, exposed themselves to infamy and suffering. The Scriptures are not the production of designing priests, or aspiring politicians, as they are in direct opposition to the interests of such men. Then, of necessity, their authors must have been honest men. If they were honest, they would relate only what they knew to be the truth. Another argument in favor of their sincerity, is, that they frankly relate their own faults and errors, and do not conceal from the world an honest avowal of the crosses, difficulties, and troubles, connected with embracing their new religion.

4. *Those writers had the means of knowing the truth of what they related, so that they could not be mistaken.* Take one circumstance for an example. Their Master raised a dead man, Lazarus.—Had he designed to impose upon their credulity, he could not in that case; for this man was raised after he had been dead four days; he lived some time afterwards and was seen by enemies as well as friends. Another relation which they gave, was, that their Leader at one time fed five thousand men, and at another seven thousand, besides all the women and children present, with a very

concerning his duty, and should be known, believed, and obeyed, without addition, deduction, or alteration. If they are able to make one wise unto salvation, perfect, and thoroughly furnished unto all good works, they reveal the will of God sufficiently to direct us in all important duties, and should be held by every Christian as his only infallible rule of faith and practice. Randall, on giving the Scriptures a critical examination, became convinced that erroneous constructions had been put upon certain portions of them by the different denominations. Hence, he and his associates, from a sense of duty, took a stand by themselves, and publicly advocated their doctrine. As other denominations receive the Scriptures as the foundation of *their* belief, it is asked, 'Does the Bible contain different systems of doctrine? If not, where is the line of distinction between the Free-will Baptists and others?' Answer. The Bible contains one, and only one, system of doc-

small portion of food; and that, after they had all satisfied their hunger, more food was taken up in fragments than there was at first. This case offered no opportunity for deception, there being so many, both foes and friends, who ate.

Then we have to a moral certainty, proved by arguments but little short of mathematical demonstration, that the Scriptures are authentic, genuine, and a divine revelation.

trine ; and this, if rightly understood, is perfectley harmonious. The line of distinction is not in the Bible, but in the different constructions put upon it by men.

3. REASONS FOR PUBLISHING THE FOLLOWING WORK. 1. As our Connexion has become so extensive that all cannot meet and confer together on doctrine as formerly, some are at a loss to know how the body understand certain portions of the Bible. Persons frequently join us who have not been educated in our sentiments, and who, in some respects, are still influenced by their former opinions. The consequence is, that, for want of proper information, some hold and teach sentiments differing from those of the body; whereas, the Bible requires us all to "speak the same thing." 2. Certain individuals, when called to account for not being sound in the faith, have taken occasion to evade, saying, "The Free-will Baptists have not published their doctrine ; but they take the Scriptures as their only rule of faith and practice. These I take ; and I have as good a right to my construction, as you have to yours ; therefore you have no authority to call me to an account; but I might as well call you to order for differing from me, as you reprove me for differing from you." 3. In

some instances, persons calling themselves Free-will Baptists have gone into places where we are little known, preached false doctrines, and prejudiced the public mind against us ; so that, on visiting those places, our preachers, for want of a suitable publication on doctrine, have found it difficult to convince the people that they had been imposed upon. 4. Many persons, on a partial acquaintance, are favorably disposed toward us, and wish to know our sentiments in general, that they may be enabled to determine whether they can unite with us. It does not satisfy such inquirers, if we say, ' We believe the doctrine of the Bible ; and if you believe that, we are in unison.' In return, they say, ' Universalists, Unitarians, &c., pretend that *they* hold to the doctrine of the Bible—do you believe as they do ?' We must answer, ' No. We believe that they construe certain portions of the Scriptures erroneously.' The inquirers still ask, ' And how do you construe them ?' If this query, which is made by thousands, be answered, something must be written. 5. A suitable Treatise, showing our faith, may be instrumental of gathering into our Connexion many independent societies, and many individuals, who believe as we do, but who, as yet, have little knowledge of our sentiments. It may also serve as an additional means of spreading the truth where our preachers have been able to labor but little. For these reasons, the Conference thought it necessary that we publish our understanding of the Scriptures.

It may be objected, that, by this publication, a stand is taken different from that at first maintained by the Free-will Baptists. We answer, it has ever been the labor of our brethren to proclaim our faith. A contrary course would be to *light a candle and place it under a bushel.* Our doctrine has been published, more or less, in every extempore sermon delivered by our preachers ; also, in printed sermons, magazines, and other periodicals. In this publication, we only do in a *connected* form, what our fathers in the church have often done in *detached* and *various* forms. It is by no means designed to form a new creed for our brethren ; our creed was formed eighteen hundred years ago. But this Treatise is designed to show our views as a denomination. It may also lead to a better understanding of the Bible. We claim no power to bind the consciences of men, or to say that any man shall believe as we do. Still, it is not expected that any will be admitted to church fellowship, whose understanding of the Scriptures varies, essentially, from ours. Nor is it expected that any brother among us will labor to propagate sentiments contrary to the general views of the body. This would *make divisions* contrary to the law of Christ.

TREATISE.

CHAPTER I.

Being and Attributes of God.

The Scriptures teach that there is only one true and living God,(*a*) who is a Spirit,(*b*) self-existent,(*c*) eter-

(*a*) 1 Cor. 8:4. There is none other God but one. Jer. 10:10. But the Lord is the true God, he is the living God. 1 John 7: 28. 2 Cor. 1:18. 1 John 5:20. Num. 13:19.

(*b*) John 4:24. God is a Spirit. 2 Cor. 3:17.

(*c*) Ex. 3:14. And God said unto Moses, I AM THAT I AM. Ps. 83:18. John 5:26. Ex. 6:3. Rev. 1:4. JEHOVAH signifies, "*He that exists of himself.*"

nal,(*d*) immutable,(*e*) omnipresent,(*f*) omniscient,(*g*) omnipotent,(*h*) independent,(*i*) good,(*j*) wise,(*k*) ho-

---

(*d*) Ps. 90:2. From everlasting to everlasting, thou art God. Deut. 33:27. 1 Tim. 1:17. Rom. 1:20. Isa. 57:15. Jer. 10:10.

(*e*) Mal. 3:6. For I am the Lord, I change not. James 1:17. Num. 23:19.

(*f*) 1 Kings 8:27. But will God indeed dwell on the earth? Behold, the heaven, and heaven of heavens, cannot contain thee. Jer. 23:24. 2 Chron. 2:6. Acts 17:14. Isa. 57:15. Ps. 139:7—12.

(*g*) Acts 15:18. Known unto God are all his works from the beginning of the world. 1 Tim. 1:17. Ps. 94:9, 10. 1 Chron. 28:9. Job. 42:2. Acts 1:24. 1 John 3:26.

(*h*) Rev. 19:6. The Lord God omnipotent reigneth. Matt. 19:26. Mark. 10:27. 14:36. Luke 18:27. Job 42:2. Ps. 135:6.

(*i*) Eph. 4:6. One God and Father of all, who is above all, and through all, and in you all. Isa. 40:13—15. Rom. 11:33—36. Job 9:12. 41:11. Dan. 4:35.

(*j*) Ps. 119:68. Thou art good, and doest good. Ps. 25:8. 86:5. 100:5. Ex. 9:27.

(*k*) Rom. 16:27. To God only wise, be glory through Jesus Christ forever. Amen. 1 Tim. 1 1:7. Jude 25. Dan. 2:20.

ly,(*l*) just,(*m*) and merciful;(*n*) the Creator,(*o*) Preserver,(*p*) and Governor,(*q*) of the universe; the Redeemer,(*r*) Savior,(*s*) Sanctifier,(*t*)

(*l*) Lev. 19:2. I the Lord your God am holy. Lev. 21:8. 11:44, 45. Job 6:10. Ps. 71:22. Isa. 1:4. 43:3.

(*m*) Ps. 119:137. Righteous art thou, O Lord, and upright are thy judgments. Deut. 32:4. Just and right is he. Ps. 92:15. Zeph. 3:5.

(*n*) Eph. 2:4, 5. God who is rich in mercy. Ps. 100:5. 103:8. Ex. 34:6. Neh. 9:17.

(*o*) Gen. 1:1. In the beginning God created the heaven and the earth. Gen. 2:5, 7. Col. 1:16. Heb. 11:3. Ps. 33:6, 9. Ex. 20:11.

(*p*) Neh. 9:6. Thou, even thou, art Lord alone; thou hast made heaven, the heaven of heavens, with all their host, the earth, and all things that are therein, the seas, and all that is therein, and thou preservest them all. Heb. 1:3. Col. 1:17. Job 7:20.

(*q*) Ps. 47:7. God is the King of all the earth. 2 Chron. 20:6. Ps. 95:3.

(*r*) Isa. 47:4 As for our Redeemer, the Lord of Hosts is his name. Isa. 41:14. 59:20. Prov. 23:11. Ps. 78:35. Jer. 50:34.

(*s*) Isa. 45:21. There is no God else besides me; a just God, and a Savior; there is none besides me. Isa. 43:3, 11. 45:15, 21. 49:26. 60:16. Hos. 13:4. John 4:42.

(*t*) Ex. 31:13. I am the Lord that doth

and Judge(*u*) of men; and the only proper object of Divine worship.(*v*)

---

sanctify you. 1 Thess. 5:23. Ezra 37:28. Heb. 13:12. Jude 1.

(*u*) Heb. 12:22, 23. Ye are come—to God the Judge of all. Gen. 18:25. Ps. 50:6. 2 Tim. 4:8.

(*v*) Ex 34:14. Thou shalt worship no other god; for the Lord, whose name is Jealous, is a jealous God. Matt. 4:10. Thou shalt worship the Lord thy God, and him only shalt thou serve. Ex. 34:14. Rev. 19:10. 22: 8, 9.

REMARKS. On surveying the world and its appendages, the proof of God's existence is strongly exhibited. The order of the planetary hosts, and the system of organized matter, assuming forms adapted to certain ends, manifestly show that there must be a contriver. This contriver must, of necessity, be self-existent; and, consequently, eternal. He is Almighty, or he could not produce and sustain the universe; and All-wise, or he could not have introduced a system of such harmony and beauty. This kind of reasoning, which some have termed proving the existence of God from the light of nature, is acknowledged by revelation. "For the invisible things of him from the creation of the world are clearly seen, being understood by

The mode of his existence, however, is a subject far above the understanding of man.(*w*) Finite beings cannot comprehend him.(*x*) There is nothing in the universe that can justly represent him, for there is none like him.(*y*) Such is the character of God. He is the fountain of all perfection and happiness. He is glorified by the whole inanimate creation, and is worthy to be loved and served by all intelligences.(*z*)

---

the things that are made, even his eternal power and God-head; so that they are without excuse." Rom. 1:20. Hence those who have not the Bible nor the preached gospel are inexcusable if they do not believe and worship God.

(*w*) Job 11:7. Canst thou by searching find out God? Isa. 40:28.

(*x*) Isa. 40:25. To whom then will ye liken me? Rom. 11:33.

(*y*) Ex. 9:14. There is none like me in all the earth. Ex. 3:14. 1 Chron. 17:20.

(*z*) Ps. 19:1, 2. The heavens declare the glory of God; and the firmament showeth his handy-work. Day unto day uttereth speech, and night unto night showeth knowledge. Ps. 150:6. Let every thing that hath breath praise the LORD. Ps. 145:10. All thy works shall praise thee.

CHAPTER II.

Creation, Primitive State of Man, and his Fall.

SECTION I.—CREATION.

1. *Of the world.* God created the world and all things that it contains, for his own pleasure and glory, and the enjoyment of his creatures.(*a*)

2. *Of the angels.* The angels were created by God(*b*) to glorify him,(*c*) and obey his commandments. (*d*)

(*a*) Rev. 4:11. Thou hast created all things, and for thy pleasure they are, and were created. Isa. 43:7. I have created him for my glory. 1 Tim. 6:17. The living God, who giveth us richly all things to enjoy.

(*b*) Col. 1:16. For by him were all things created that are in heaven, and that are in earth, visible and invisible.

(*c*) Rev. 7:11. And all the angels stood round about,—and fell before the throne on their faces and worshipped God.

(*d*) Ps. 103:20. Bless the Lord, ye his angels,—that do his commandments.

Those who have kept their first estate,* he employs in ministering blessings to the heirs of salvation,(*e*) and in executing his judgments upon the world.(*f*)

3. *Of man.* God created man, consisting of a coporeal body and a thinking, rational soul.(*g*) He was made in the similitude of God to glorify his Maker.(*h*)

(*e*) Heb. 1:14. Are they not all ministering spirits, sent forth to minister for them who shall be heirs of salvation. Dan. 6:22.

(*f*) 2 Sam. 24:16. The angel stretched out his hand upon Jerusalem to destroy it. Rev. 16:1.

(*g*) Gen. 2:7. And the Lord God formed man of the dust of the ground, and breathed into his nostrils the breath of life; and man became a living soul. Matt. 2:11.

(*h*) Gen. 1:27. So God created man in his own image; in the image of God created he him. 1 Cor. 11:7. Man—is the image and glory of God.

---

*Jude 6. And the angels which kept not their first estate, but left their own habitation, he hath reserved in everlasting chains under darkness, unto the judgment of the great day.

SECTION II.—PRIMITIVE STATE OF MAN AND HIS FALL.

Our first parents, in their original state of probation, were perfectly righteous: they naturally preferred and desired to obey their Creator, and had no preference or desire to transgress his will, (*a*) till they were deceived, inclined, and influenced by the tempter,

---

(*a*) Eccl. 7:29. God hath made man upright. Gen. 1:27. God created man in his own image. Eph. 4:24. Col. 3:10.

REMARKS. This image cannot be the body of man, as God has no definable configuration with which it can be compared. But it can be traced, 1. *In his intellectual powers.* God is an intelligent, indivisible, immaterial, and self-directing existent, who possesses a will, judgment and memory. In these respects, the soul of man was made in the image of God. The soul is *intelligent*, or capable of receiving and imparting knowledge; *indivisible*, or not capable of being separated into parts; and *immaterial*, or not composed of matter. It is a self-directing existence, as it has the power of determining how to act when different motives are placed before it. It also has the power of originating motives. Hence man is a free, moral agent; and accountable to his Maker as such. He possess-

to disobey God's commands. Previously to this, the only tendency of their nature was to do righteousness. In consequence of the first transgression, the state of trial, under which the posterity of Adam come into the world, is so far different from that of Adam, that they have not that righteousness and purity which Adam had by creation; are not naturally willing to obey God, but prefer to disobey him, and are naturally inclined to evil rather

---

es a will, memory and judgment. God can exist independently of matter, so can the soul of man. Matt. 10:28. 25:46. 22:32. 2. *In his moral qualities.* His intellectual powers and his passions were duly tempered, so that they were free from every thing improper, low, base, mean, or sinful. This image consists in knowledge, righteousness, and true holiness. Eph. 4:24. Col. 3:10. From this it may be inferred, that man in his primitive state was wise in his mind, holy in his heart, and righteous in his actions. Man, thus created, was placed in a state of probation, under a law, which he was required to keep. Gen. 2:16 17. As he was a free moral agent, he had ability to keep the law and live, or disobey and suffer its penalties.

than good.(*b*) Hence, none, by virtue of any natural goodness, can become the holy children of God:(*c*) but they are all dependent for salvation upon the redemption effected through the blood of Christ, and upon being created anew unto holiness through the op-

(*b*) Ps. 51:5. Behold I was shapen in iniquity; and in sin did my mother conceive me. Job 14:4. Who can bring a clean thing out of an unclean? not one. Job 15:14. What is man, that he should be clean? and he which is born of a woman, that he should be righteous? John 3:6. That which is born of the flesh is flesh; and that which is born of the Spirit is spirit. Ps. 58:3. The wicked are estranged from the womb; they go astray as soon as they be born, speaking lies. Gen. 8:21. For the imagination of man's heart is evil from his youth. Rom. 5:12—19. Wherefore, as by one man, sin entered into the world, and death by sin; and so death passed upon all men, for that all have sinned. For as by one man's disobedience many were made sinners. Eccl. 7:20. Prov. 22:15. Isa. 48:8. Rom. 8:7. Gen. 6:5.

(*c*) John 6:44. No man can come unto me, except the Father, which hath sent me, draw him. 1 Cor. 2:14. The natural man receiveth not the things of the Spirit of God; for they are foolishness unto him: neither can

eration of the Spirit;(*d*) both of which are freely provided for every descendant of Adam.(*e*)

CHAPTER III.

Of Christ.

SECTION I.

The Son of God possesses all Divine perfections. As he and the Father are one, he, in his Divine character, performed all the offices and works

---

he know them. Jer. 17:9. The heart is deceitful above all things, and desperately wicked: who can know it? Rom. 3:9—23. 8:8. John 15:5. Eph. 2:9. 2 Tim. 1:9.

(*d*) Rom. 5:18. As by the offence of one, judgment came upon all men to condemnation; even so by the righteousness of one, the free gift came upon all men unto justification of life. Col. 1:14. In whom we have redemption through his blood, even the forgiveness of sin. John 3:3. Except a man be born again, he cannot see the kingdom of God. Heb. 12:14. Without holinesss, no man shall see the Lord. 2 Cor. 5:10. Titus 3:5.

(*e*) *See Atonement.*

of God to his creatures, that have been the subjects of revelation to us. As man, he performed all the duties toward God that we are required to perform, the repentance of sin and from dead works excepted.

His Divine perfections are proved from his titles, his attributes, and his works.

1. *His titles.* The Bible ascribes to Christ the titles of Savior,(*a*) Jeho-

---

(*a*) Isa. 45:21, 22. There is no God else besides me; a just God, and a Savior: there is none besides me. Look unto me, and be ye saved, all the ends of the earth; for I am God, and there is none else. Hos. 13:4. I am the Lord thy God—and thou shalt know no God but me: for there is no Savior besides me. Isa. 43:10, 11. Before me there was no God formed, neither shall there be after me. I, even I, am the Lord; and besides me there is no Savior. That there is no Savior but Jehovah, is evident from the texts just quoted. From the following, it is equally evident that *Christ* is that Savior, and of course possesses the highest Divine perfections: Now we believe, not because of thy saying; for we have heard him ourselves, and know that this is indeed the Christ, the Sa-

·ah,(*b*) Lord of Hosts,(*c*) the First

---

ior of the world. John 4:42. See also Acts
:12. 5:31. Eph. 5:23. Phil. 3:20. 2 Tim. 1:
0. Titus 1:4. 2:13. 3:6. 2 Pet. 1:11.

(*b*) Isa. 40:3. The voice of him that crieth
n the wilderness, Prepare ye the way of the
ORD, [*Jehovah*,] make straight in the des-
rt a highway for our God. Luke 1:76. And
hou, child,—shalt go before the face of the
ord, to prepare his ways. Compare Ps. 68:
7, 18, with Eph. 4:7, 8. Jer. 23:6, and 1
Cor. 1:30.—Isa. 42:8. See also Rev. 1:8.—
Compare Joel 2:32 with Rom. 10:3—13; also
Ex. 6:3, and Gen. 17:1, with Ex. 3:2, 4. Isa.
3:9. Mal. 3:1, and Rom. 10:4—9. Lord, in
he Old Testament, when it occurs in small
apitals, signifies JEHOVAH. This is God's
ncommunicable name, and he has declared,
Isa. 48:8,) that he will not give his glory to
nother. Ps. 83:18. Whose name ALONE is
EHOVAH.

(*c*) Isa. 8:13, 14. Sanctify the Lord of
osts himself; and let him be your fear, and
et him be your dread. And he shall be for
sanctuary; but for a stone of stumbling,
nd for a rock of offence, to both the houses
f Israel. This passage is applied to Christ,
Pet. 2:4—6. To whom coming, as unto
living stone, disallowed indeed of men, but
hosen of God, and precious,—Wherefore al-
o it is contained in the Scripture, Behold, I

and the Last,(*d*) God,(*e*) true God,(*f*)

---

lay in Sion a chief corner stone. See also Eph. 2:20—2. Matt. 21:22. Compare also Isa. 6:5, with John 12:41. Then said I, wo is me!—for mine eyes have seen the King, the LORD of hosts. These things said Esaias when he saw his [Christ's] glory, and spake of him. Ps. 24:7—10.

(*d*) Rev. 22:13. I am Alpha and Omega the beginning and the end, the first and the last. Compare Rev. 1:8 with Isa. 44:6. I am the first, and the last; and besides me there is no God. Rev. 1:11. 21:6. 22:13.

(*e*) 1 Tim. 3:16. God was manifest in the flesh. Acts 20:28. Feed the church of God which he hath purchased with his own blood 1 John 3:16. Hereby perceive we the love of God, because he laid down his life for us Jude 25. To the only wise God our Savior be glory and majesty, dominion and power John 1:1. And the Word was God. John 20 28, 29. And Thomas answered and said unto him, My Lord, and my God. Jesus saith unto him, Thomas, because thou hast seen me, thou hast believed: blessed are they that have not seen, and yet have believed Heb. 1:8. But unto the Son, he saith, thy throne, O God, is forever and ever, &c. Col. 2:9. Tit. 2:10. Heb. 3:4.

(*f*) 1 John 5:20. We are in him that is true, even in his Son Jesus Christ. This is the true God and eternal life. Jer. 10:10, 11

great God,(*g*) God over all,(*h*) Mighty God, and the everlasting Father.(*i*)

2. *His attributes.* He is eternal,(*j*)

(*g*) Titus 2:13. Looking for that blessed hope, and the glorious appearing of the great God, and our Savior Jesus Christ. The Scriptures do not teach that the *Father* will appear to judge the world; but that this will be the work of Christ. See Rev. 22:12. 2 Thess. 1:7—10. 2 Tim. 4:1.

(*h*) Rom. 9:5. Of whom, as concerning the flesh, Christ came, who is over all, God blessed forever. Amen.

(*i*) Isa. 9:6. His name shall be called,—The mighty God, the everlasting Father. The Scriptures teach that there is but *one* true God. Isa. 45:5. I am the Lord, and there is none else, there is no God besides me. And as they teach that Jesus Christ is truly God, the conclusion necessarily follows, that the Father and Son, though two in person, are but one being. Should this proposition appear difficult to any, they may solve it by reflecting that two persons of infinite perfections cannot exist separately and distinctly, so as to constitute two beings.

(*j*) Col. 1:17. And he is before all things. Mic. 5:2. Whose goings forth have been from of old, from everlasting. Heb. 1:8. But unto the Son he saith, Thy throne, O God, is forever and ever. If his throne is forever and ever, he himself must be forever and ever.

unchangeable,(*k*) omnipresent,(*l*) omniscient, (*m*) omnipotent, (*n*) ho-

See John 1:1. 8:58. Prov. 8:22—32. Heb. 1 12. 13:8. Rev. 1:8, 17, 18. 17:5, 24.

(*k*) Heb. 13:8. Jesus Christ, the same yesterday, and to-day, and forever. Heb. 1:12 Thou art the same, and thy years shall not fail. 2 Tim. 2:19.

(*l*) John 3:13. No man hath ascended up to heaven, but he that came down from heaven, even the Son of Man, which is in heaven. From this it is seen that Christ is at the same time on earth and in heaven. Matt. 28:20. Lo, I am with you alway, even unto the end of the world. For where two or three are gathered together in my name, there am I in the midst of them. See Eph. 1:23.

(*m*) Rev. 2:23. And all the churches shall know that I am he which searcheth the reins and hearts. *Hence he knows the hearts of all* John 2:24, 25. But Jesus did not commit himself unto them, because he knew all men and needed not that any should testify of man: for he knew what was in man. John 16:30. We are sure that thou knowest all things. John 1:18. 10:15. 21:27. Acts 1:24.

(*n*) Col. 2:8, 10. Christ—is the head of all principality and power. Ps. 45:3. Gird thy sword upon thy thigh, O most Mighty, with thy glory and thy majesty. Compare this with verse 2 and Rev. 19:16. Matt. 28:

ly,(*o*) and is entitled to Divine worship.(*p*)

---

18. All power is given unto me in heaven and in earth. 1 Cor. 1 : 24. 15 : 24, 25. John 10 : 18. 17 : 2. Eph. 1 : 21. Heb. 1 : 3. Christ declares that He is "Almighty." Rev. 1 : 8. 1 Cor. 4 : 5.

(*o*) Acts 3 : 14. But ye denied the Holy One and the Just. Mark 1 : 24. Luke 1 : 35. Heb. 7 : 26. Rev. 3 : 7.

(*p*) *The angels are required to worship him.* Heb. 1:6. Let all the angels of God worship him. *All men are required to worship him.* John 5:23. That all men should honor the Son, even as they honor the Father. Phil. 2:10, 11. That at the name of Jesus every knee should bow, of things in heaven, and things in earth, and things under the earth; and that every tongue should confess, that Jesus Christ is Lord, to the glory of God the Father. *He received worship from his followers and others.* Matt. 28:9. And they came and held him by the feet and worshipped him. Luke 24:52. And they worshipped him, and returned to Jerusalem with great joy. Matt. 2:2. 8:2. 9:18. 28:19. John 9:38. Rev. 1:5, 6. 5:9—14. 7:9, 10. 2 Peter 3:18. Gal. 1:5. 1 Cor. 1:2. 2 Cor. 13:14. *Prayer was made to him.* Acts 7:59, 60. And they stoned Stephen, calling upon God and saying, Lord Jesus, receive my spirit. And he kneeled down, and cried with a loud voice,

3. *His works.* By Christ, the world was created; (*q*) he pre-

Lord, lay not this sin to their charge. 1 Cor. 1:2. Acts 1:24.

NOTE. Since Jehovah requires all men to worship him, and makes it idolatry to worship any other being, it would surely be idolatry to worship Christ, if he did not possess the perfections of Jehovah. Yet Christ claimed Divine worship, and holy saints worshipped him.

(*q*) Heb. 1:8, 10. Unto the Son he saith, 'Thou, Lord, in the beginning hast laid the foundation of the earth; and the heavens are the works of thine hands.' John 1:3, 10. All things were made by him [Christ]; and without him was not anything made that was made. The world was made by him. Col. 1:16. For by him were all things created that are in heaven and that are in earth. The fact, that God made the world *by* Jesus Christ, gives no reason for the conclusion that Christ is not the Creator of all things; for 'he and the Father are one,' and 'what things soever he [the Father] doeth, these also doeth the Son likewise.' John 5:19. See also Eph. 3:9. 1 Cor. 8:6. Heb. 3:3, 4. And though God did the work BY Jesus Christ, it was nevertheless *by himself*, as may be seen from Isa. 44:24. 45:12. I am the Lord (Jehovah) that maketh all things, that stretcheth forth the heavens *alone*, that spread-

serves (*r*) and governs it; (*s*) he has redeemed men, (*t*) and he

---

eth abroad the earth BY MYSELF. I have made the earth, and created man upon it. I, even *my hands*, have stretched out the heavens, and all their hosts have I commanded. The work of creation being ascribed to Christ, the conclusion follows that his person is Divine, for, "He that built all things is God." Heb. 3:4. Again, it is written, 2 Kings 19: 15, O LORD GOD of Israel,—thou art the God, even thou alone,—thou hast made heaven and earth.

(*r*) Heb. 1:3. Who, being the brightness of his glory, and the express image of his person, and upholding all things by the word of his power. Col. 1:17. And he is before all things, and by him all things consist. Matt. 28:18.

(*s*) Isa. 9:6. The government shall be upon his shoulder. If Christ were not God, if he did not possess infinite perfections, no mere delegated power could enable him to uphold, preserve, and govern all things. For the infinite *capacity* and *perfections* of God, are essential to the universal preservation and government. 1 Pet. 3:22. Col. 2:10. Eph. 1:21. 1 Cor. 15:24.

(*t*) Eph. 1:7. In whom we have redemption through his blood, the forgiveness of sins. Heb. 9:12. Having obtained eternal redemption for us. Isa. 54:5. For thy Maker is thine husband; the LORD of hosts is his

will be their final Judge.(*u*)

---

name; and thy redeemer, the Holy One of Israel; the God of the whole earth shall he be called. Gal. 3:13. Christ hath redeemed us from the curse of the law. Ps. 19:14. 78:35. Isa. 43:14. 44:6. 49:26. 60:16. Jer. 50:34. Gal. 4:4, 5. 1 Pet. 1:18, 19. Tit. 2:14. Rev. 5:9.

(*u*) 2 Tim. 4:1. The Lord Jesus Christ—shall judge the quick and the dead at his appearing. Matt. 25:31—46. John 5:22. For the Father judgeth no man, but hath committed all judgment unto the Son. From other scriptures, it appears that "God is judge himself." Ps. 50:6. 75:7. Heb. 12:23, and that the LORD (Jehovah) will judge the world. 1 Chron. 16:33. Ps. 82:8. 96:13. Jon 5:27. Acts 10:42. Rom. 2:16. Rev. 1:7.

NOTE. By comparing the Scriptures quoted, it is evident that the attributes and works of God are indiscriminately ascribed to Christ, consequently a unity exists between the Father and Son, which constitutes but one being. To this agreeth the testimony of John 1:1, 3, 14. In the beginning was the Word, and the Word was with God, and the Word was God. All things were made by him; and without him was not anything made that was made. And the Word was made flesh and dwelt among us. And Christ saith, John 10:30, I and my Father are one.

SECTION II.—THE INCARNATION OF CHRIST.

The Word, which in the beginning was with God, and which was God, by whom all things were made, condescended to a state of humiliation in becoming united with human nature, or a body like ours, pollution and sin excepted. (*a*) In this state, as a subject

(*a*) John 1:14. And the Word was made flesh and dwelt among us. 1 Tim. 3:16. God was manifest in the flesh. Phil. 2:6, 7, 8. Who, being in the form of God, thought it not robbery to be equal with God; but made himself of no reputation, and took upon him the form of a servant, and was made in the likeness of man: And being found in fashion as a man, he humbled himself, and became obedient unto death, even the death of the cross. Heb. 2:14, 16. Forasmuch then as the children are partakers of flesh and blood, he also himself likewise took part of the same. —For verily he took not on him the nature of angels: but he took on him the seed of Abraham. Gal. 4:4. God sent forth his Son, made of a woman, made under the law.— Luke 2:52. And Jesus increased in wisdom and stature. 2 Cor. 8:9. Isa. 9:6. Heb. 10:5.

of the law, he was liable to all the infirmities of our nature ;(*b*) was tempted as we are ;(*c*) but lived our example,(*d*) and rendered perfect obedience to the Divine requirements.(*e*) As Christ was made of the seed of David according to the flesh, he is called "*The* Son of Man ;"(*f*)* and as the

(*b*) Matt. 8:17. Himself took our infirmities and bare our sicknesses. Heb. 2:17. Wherefore in all things, it behooved him to be made like unto his brethren. Matt. 4:2. 21:18. 27:50. John 6:6. 19:28. 11:33, 35. Isa. 53:3. Matt. 8:24. Luke 22:44.

(*c*) Heb. 4:15. But was in all points tempted like as we are, yet without sin. Matt. 4:1—11.

(*d*) 1 Pet. 2:21. Because Christ also suffered for us, leaving an example, that ye should follow his steps. Rom. 15:5, 6.

(*e*) Isa. 42:21. He will magnify the law, and make it honorable. Matt. 5:17. 3:15. Gal. 4:4.

(*f*) Luke 19:10. For the Son of Man is come to seek and to save that which was lost.

---

* Some have said that Christ is called "THE *Son of man*," by way of *eminence*, he being the only person thus distinguished in the Scriptures.

Divine existence is the fountain from which he proceeded, and was the only agency by which his body was begotten,(*g*) he is called the Son of God;(*h*) being the only begotten of the Father,(*i*) and the only incarnation of the Divine Being.

(*g*) John 16:27, 28. I came out from God. Matt. 1:18, 20.

(*h*) Luke 1:35. That holy thing which shall be born of thee, shall be called the Son of God.

(*i*) John 3:16. For God so loved the world that he gave his only begotten Son. 1 John 4:9. John 1:18.

Remarks. Some contend that Christ is inferior to the Father, and to prove this, they quote Mark 13:32. "But of that day, and that hour, knoweth no man, no, not the angels which are in heaven, neither the Son, but the Father." If this passage signifies that the knowledge of Christ was limited, it plainly contradicts others already quoted, which prove that he is omniscient. But considering the word *know* to have the same meaning here that it has in 1 Cor. 2:2, "For I determined not to know anything among you, save Jesus Christ, and him crucified," it involves no obscurity; for it there has the causative sense, 'I determined not *to cause to know* or *make known*,' &c. By examining the

CHAPTER IV.

Holy Spirit.

1. The Scriptures ascribe to the Holy Ghost the acts and attributes of

---

whole chapter, it appears that Christ gave a very circumstantial account of the *event itself* and the facts attending and following it. Of course, he possessed a much greater amount of knowledge than was needful simply to understand the *time*, which, for important reasons, was not as yet to be announced. By the text, then, we are taught that neither Christ, nor the apostles, nor any man, will make known by prophecy, or in any other way, the *time* of this event; and that it shall be made known only by the providences of God which accompany it.

Again, they urge his inferiority from John 5:19. The Son can do nothing of himself. But it should be observed, that the controversy between Christ and the Jews, did not relate to his *power*, but to the *lawfulness* of his acts. The Jews charged him with two crimes—violating the Sabbath, and claiming equality with God. In reply, Christ said that he could do nothing of himself, except what the Father did; and that what things soever were done by the Father, were likewise performed

an intelligent being. He is said to

---

by the Son. The meaning of the passage appears to be, that such is the unity between the Father and Son, that the latter cannot act without the former. Consequently, it is one of the strongest proofs of his Divinity. Some have ridiculed the idea that one class of Scriptures relates to the Divinity of Christ, and others only to his humanity. There is, however, no reason for this contempt; since this manner of speaking has ever been common with the best writers in every language. When it is said that a *man walks*, there is no allusion to an exercise of the mind; and when it is said, *he thinks*, it is not supposed that a bodily exercise is intended. Perhaps one half that has ever been written or spoken of man, if he has two natures, matter and spirit, must be understood on precisely the same principle. Why, then, should this mode of expression, when applied to the Divine Being, become a subject of ridicule?

Again, some have said that Christ cannot be the *true God*, because he is called *his Son*. But this conclusion cannot be fairly made on *their own* principle of his being *properly* the Son of God; since one nature begets the same nature, and every species begets the same species. It has been further said, "If, as a son of man is man, so the Son of God is God, it must follow, that, as a father and son are two men, so the Divine Father and his only begotten Son must be two beings, and

guide,(*a*) to know,(*b*) to move,(*c*) to give information,(*d*) to command,(*e*)

---

of course two Gods.' But any rational person may see that this reasoning is false, by considering, first, that the reason why a father and son are two beings, is, they are *finite* and *local;* and, secondly, the reason why the Divine Father and his only begotten Son are but one Being, is, their nature and attributes, being the same, are *infinite* and consequently can neither be *local* nor *limited;* but what one knows the other knows, and the mind of one is the mind of the other.

(*a*) John 16:13. Howbeit, when he, the Spirit of truth, is come, he will guide you into all truth.

(*b*) 1 Cor. 2:11. Even so the things of God knoweth no man, but the Spirit of God.

(*c*) Gen. 1:2. And the Spirit of God moved upon the face of the waters. Acts 8 : 39.—And when they were come up out of the water, the Spirit of the Lord caught away Philip, that the eunuch saw him no more

(*d*) Acts 21:11. And when he was come unto us, he took Paul's girdle, and bound his own hands and feet, and said, Thus saith the Holy Ghost, so shall the Jews at Jerusalem, bind the man, &c. Acts 10:19. While Peter thought on the vision, the Spirit said unto him, Behold, three men seek thee. John 16:14, 15. John 14:26.

(*e*) Acts 13:2. The Holy Ghost said, sepa-

to forbid,(*f*) to send forth,(*g*) to reprove,(*h*) and to be sinned against.(*i*)

2. The attributes of God are applied to the Holy Ghost; such as eternity,(*j*) omnipresence,(*k*) omnis-

---

rate me Barnabas and Saul for the work whereunto I have called them.

(*f*) Acts 16:6. Now when they had gone throughout Phrygia, and the region of Galatia, and were forbidden of the Holy Ghost to preach the word in Asia.

(*g*) Acts 13:4. So they, being sent forth by the Holy Ghost, departed unto Selucia.

(*h*) John 16:8 And when he is come, he will reprove the world of sin, and of righteousness, and of judgment. Gen. 6:3.

(*i*) Matt. 12:32. But whosoever speaketh against the Holy Ghost, it shall not be forgiven him, neither in this world, neither in the world to come. Isa. 63:10. Acts 7:51. Acts 5:3, 4, 9. Eph. 4:30. 1 Thess. 5:19. *Were the Holy Ghost only an attribute of God, this unpardonable sin could not be committed against him. For though man can sin against an individual, he cannot sin against one of his attributes, abstractly considered.*

(*j*) Heb. 9:14. How much more shall the blood of Christ, who through the eternal Spirit offered himself without spot to God purge your conscience from dead works.

(*k*) Ps. 139:7. Whither shall I go from thy

cience,(*l*) goodness,(*m*) and truth.(*n*)

3. The works of God are ascribed to the Holy Ghost; creation,(*o*) inspiration,(*p*) giving of life,(*q*) and sanctification.(*r*)

Spirit? or whither shall I flee from thy presence?

(*l*) 1 Cor. 2:10, 11. But God hath revealed them unto us by his Spirit; for the Spirit searcheth all things, yea, the deep things of God. Even so the things of God knoweth no man, but the Spirit of God.

(*m*) Neh. 9:20. Thou gavest also thy good Spirit to instruct them. Ps. 143:10.

(*n*) John 14:17. Even the Spirit of truth, whom the world cannot receive, because it seeth him not.

(*o*) Job 26:13. By his Spirit he hath garnished the heavens. Job 33:4. The Spirit of God hath made me, and the breath of the Almighty hath given me life. Ps. 104:30. Thou sendeth forth thy Spirit, they are created.

(*p*) 2 Pet. 1:21. Prophecy came not in old time by the will of man; but holy men of God spake as they were moved by the Holy Ghost. Acts 28:25.

(*q*) 1 Pet. 3:18. For Christ also hath once suffered for sins—that he might bring us to God, being put to death in the flesh, but quickened by the Spirit. John 6:23.

(*r*) 1 Cor. 6:11. But ye are sanctified, but ye are justified, in the name of the Lord Je-

4. The same acts, which in one part of the Bible are attributed to the Holy Ghost, are in other parts said to be performed by God.(*s*)

5. The apostles assert that the

sus, and by the Spirit of our God. Romans 15:16.

GOD.

(*s*) Isa. 6:8, 9. I heard the voice of the Lord, saying, Whom shall I send, and who will go for us? Then I said, here am I; send me. And he said, Go, and tell this people, Hear ye indeed, but understand not; and see ye indeed, but perceive not.

In several places Christ is called the only begotten Son of God. See also Dan. 2:20. Ps. 62:11. Isa. 48:16. Eph. 4:11. John 6:45. Isa. 48:17.

SPIRIT.

Acts 28:25, 26. Well spake the Holy Ghost by Esaias the prophet unto our fathers, saying, Go unto this people, and say, Hearing ye shall hear, and not understand; and seeing, ye shall see, and not perceive.

Matt. 1:18. Now the birth of Jesus Christ was on this wise; When as his mother Mary was espoused to Joseph, before they came together, she was found with child of the Holy Ghost.—See also Isa. 11 : 2. Rom: 15:13. Isa. 48:16. Acts 13:4. John 14:26. Rom. 8:11.

Holy Ghost is Lord and God.(*t*)

From the foregoing, the conclusion is, that the Holy Ghost is in reality God, and one with the Father in all Divine perfections. It has also been shown that Jesus Christ is God, one in essence with the Father. Then in essence these three, the Father, Son, and Holy Ghost, are one: though they are three in respect to their agency and relation to man. Hence the words found in 1 John 5:7 are true: "For there are three that bear record in heaven, the Father, the Word, and the Holy Ghost; and these three are one."

The truth of this doctrine is also proved from the fact that the Father, Son, and Holy Ghost, are united in the authority by which believers are baptized, and in the benedictions pronounced by the apostles,(*u*) which are acts of

(*t*) 2 Cor. 3:17. Now the Lord is that Spirit; and where the Spirit of the Lord is, there is liberty. Acts 5:3, 4. Why hath Satan filled thine heart to lie to the Holy Ghost?—Thou hast not lied unto man but unto God.

(*u*) Matt. 28:19. Go ye, therefore, and

the highest religious worship.

---

teach all nations, baptizing them in the name of the Father, and of the Son, and of the Holy Ghost. 2 Cor. 13:14. The grace of the Lord Jesus Christ, and the love of God, and the communion of the Holy Ghost, be with you all.

REMARKS. The term persons is used to express the threefold subsistence or distinction in the God-head, because distinct personal attributes and acts are ascribed to the Father, Son, and Holy Ghost, and because the three personal pronouns, *I*, *Thou* and *He*, with some of their variations, are in Scripture applied to them. Jer. 17:10. Heb. 1:10. John 16:13. Gen. 1:26. Its meaning, however, when applied to the Father, Son, and Holy Ghost, is not the same in all respects, as when applied to men, yet no better term can be found to convey our ideas. The soul and body of man are distinct, though they are not separate in this life, so the persons in the God-head are distinct, yet they are not separate.

But, says an objector, how can the Father, Son, and Holy Ghost, be at the same time *one* and *three*? I do not understand it; therefore I cannot believe this doctrine. But shall we not believe the existence of a thing, state, or relation, unless we can perfectly comprehend it? If not, we must disbelieve the existence of everything both material and immaterial. How does the grass grow? How

CHAPTER V.

Atonement and Mediation of Christ.*

1. ATONEMENT. As sin cannot be pardoned without a sacrifice, and the blood of beasts could never actually wash away sin, Christ gave his life a sacrifice for the sins of the world,(*a*)

---

do we come into being, and live, see, hear, remember, &c.? These are mysteries far above the comprehension of man, as well as the existence of Deity. There are thousands that cannot comprehend the laws of Newton; yet would it not be presumption in such, to say, that these laws are not true, because they do not understand them? Newton himself could understand the truth of his system. The same may be said in relation to the existence of God. It is wholly above the understanding of short-sighted man, but God can comprehend it, and has revealed the truth in his word. Though this doctrine is above reason, it is not contrary to reason; and it is wisdom in us, fallible creatures, wrapped in the darkness of the fall, to bow to the instructions of Heaven.

(*a*) 1 John 2:2. He is the propitiation for

---

* *Atonement* signifies an *expiation for sin; redemption* signifies *deliverance from sin.*

and thus made salvation possible for all men.(*b*) He died for us, suffering

---

our sins; and not for ours only, but also for the sins of the whole world. Isa. 53:5, 10, 11. But he was wounded for our transgressions, he was bruised for our iniquities; the chastisement of our peace was upon him; and with his stripes we are healed. Yet it pleased the Lord to bruise him, he hath put him to grief; when thou shall make his soul an offering for sin, he shall see his seed, and the pleasure of the Lord shall prosper in his hands. By his knowledge shall my righteous servant justify many; for he shall bear their iniquities. Rom. 4:25. Who was delivered for our offences. Matt. 20:28. The Son of Man came—to give his life a ransom for many. 1 Pet. 3:18. For Christ also hath once suffered for sins, the just for the unjust, that he might bring us to God, being put to death in the flesh. John 1:29. Behold the Lamb of God, which taketh away the sins of the world! Heb. 9:26. Gal. 1:4. Tit. 2:14. Eph. 5:25. Rom. 5:6, 8.

(*b*) Heb. 2:9. That he, by the grace of God, should taste death for every man. 1 Tim. 2:6. Who gave himself a ransom for all. Tit. 2:11. For the grace of God that bringeth salvation hath appeared to all men. Rev. 22:17. Whosoever will, let him take of the water of life freely. Isa. 45:22. Look unto me, and be ye saved, all the ends of the earth. 2 Pet. 3:9. The Lord—is long suffering to us-ward,

the penalty of the law in our stead, to make known the righteousness of God, that he might be just in justifying sinners who believe in his Son.(*c*) Through the redemption effected by Christ, salvation is actually enjoyed in this world, and will be enjoyed in the next, by all who do not in this life refuse obedience to the known requirements of God.(*d*) As for the body, no

not willing that any should perish, but that all should come to repentance. Acts 17:30. But now [God] commandeth all men every where to repent. 2 Cor. 5:14, 15. Ps. 145:9. 1 Tim. 2:3, 4. 4:10. Isa. 55:1, 7. Ps. 86:15.

(*c*) Rom. 3:25, 26. Whom God hath set forth to be a propitiation, through faith in his blood, to declare his righteousness for the remission of sins that are past, through the forbearance of God; To declare—his righteousness: that he might be just, and the justifier of him which believeth in Jesus. Rom. 13:39. 5:9, 18. Matt. 26:28. Eph. 1:7. Col. 1:14, 20. Heb. 1:3. 9:14, 22. Rev. 5:9.

(*d*) Rom. 5:18. Therefore, as by the offence of one, judgment came upon all men to condemnation; even so by the righteousness of one, the free gift came upon all men unto justification of life. Rom. 8:1. There is, therefore, now no condemnation to them which are in Christ Jesus, who walk not after

provision was made for its redemption from the consequences of the fall, till

---

the flesh, but after the Spirit. Rom. 4:15. For where no law is, there is no transgression. Luke 18:16. Suffer little children to come unto me,—for of such is the kingdom of God. Rom. 2:14.

REMARKS. From these scriptures, the following conclusions appear evident: 1. That God has actually given power to every man to obtain salvation: otherwise, Christ must have died for many, intentionally, in vain. 2. The grace or favor which God shows to all men, is sufficient for their obtaining salvation, and it will finally effect the redemption of all who do not mis-improve the favors which they receive. 3. Every sinner, through *grace*, *can* come to Christ, and partake of the water of life. Had anything less than this been intended, our Lord would not have said, "*Let him that is athirst come,*" since the wicked, who "spend their labor for that which satisfieth not," are the very persons who thirst (Isa. 55:1, 2;) but the regenerate having already come to Christ, have a well of *water in them*, and shall never thirst. John 4:14. Infants are free from personal condemnation, and those which die before they are capable of knowing good and evil will be happy; yet their happiness will not be the result of any goodness which they inherit from their parents, but of the reconciliation through the blood of Christ, by which they are renew-

the resurrection.(*e*) Then the bodies of the saints will be raised, and made like the body of Christ.(*f*) An atonement for sin was necessary.(*g*) For

---

ed in righteousness and true holiness, after the image of God.

(*e*) Rom. 8:21—23. Because the creature itself shall be delivered from the bondage of corruption, into the glorious liberty of the children of God. For we know that the whole creation groaneth and travaileth in pain together until now. And not only they, but ourselves also, which have the first-fruits of the Spirit, even we ourselves groan within ourselves, waiting for the adoption, to wit, the redemption of our body. Eph. 1:4.

(*f*) Phil. 3:21. Who shall change our vile body, that it may be fashioned like unto his glorious body. 1 Cor. 15:49, 52—54.

(*g*) Heb. 9:22. Without shedding of blood, is no remission. Eph. 1:7. In whom we have redemption through his blood, the forgiveness of sins. Rom. 5:19. For as by one man's disobedience many were made sinners; so by the obedience of one shall many be made righteous. John 1:16. Matt. 26:39.

REMARKS. Some have objected to the doctrine of the atonement, saying, "Justice cannot be satisfied by the innocent suffering for the guilty; for in this case, the criminal is cleared, and the innocent punished unrighteously." Though this objection may gener-

present and future obedience can no more blot our past sins, than past obedience can remove the guilt of present and future sins. Had God pardoned the sins of men without satisfaction for the violation of his law, it would follow that transgression might go on with impunity; government would be abrogated, and the obligation of subjection to God would be, in effect, cancelled.

2. MEDIATION OF CHRIST. Our Lord not only died for our sins, but he arose for our justification, (*h*) and as-

---

ally apply to the administration of human laws, it cannot justly apply to the case under consideration; because in this all the circumstances are very different: and many of them are so far beyond our comprehension, that we cannot be suitable judges. The principle of the innocent suffering voluntarily in room of the guilty, is not, however, without an example. The common sympathies of humanity require it to be exercised in unnumbered circumstances, and were the principle to be rejected, and rigid justice administered in all the associations of imperfect men, the miseries of the world would make life an insupportable burden.

(*h*) Rom. 4:25. Who was delivered for our

cended to heaven,(*i*) where as mediator between God and man, he will make intercession for us till the final judgment.(*j*)

---

offences, and was raised again for our justification. 1 Cor. 15:17.

(*i*) Acts 1:11. This same Jesus, which is taken up from you into heaven. Eph. 4:8. Mark 16:19.

(*j*) Heb. 9:24. Christ is—entered—into heaven itself, now to appear in the presence of God for us. 1 Tim. 2:5. For there is one God, and one mediator between God and men, the man Christ Jesus. Heb. 7:25. He ever liveth to make intercession for us. Rom. 8:34. Christ—is even at the right hand of God, who also maketh intercession for us. 1 Cor. 15:24. Then cometh the end, when he shall have delivered up the kingdom to God, even the Father. Isa. 53:12.

REMARKS. Though the sinner's boasted pride may lead him to look upon his transgressions as mere trifles, and to think that he can approach God without an intercessor—and though he may not be well pleased that his rebellion should be stamped with eternal infamy, by the necessity of the atonement and the intercession; yet, when he is truly humbled under a sense of his guilt, he scarcely dares look up towards heaven; and in the bitterness of his soul, he inquires, "Who will plead for me?"

CHAPTER VI.

The Gospel Call.

By virtue of the atonement, which is designed to counteract the effects of the fall, man is placed in a salvable state ;(*a*) the grace of God, (*b*) the influences of the Holy Spirit, (*c*) and the invitations of the gospel, are given to

---

(*a*) Matt. 18:11. For the Son of man is come to save that which was lost. John 17:4. I have finished the work which thou gavest me to do. Gal. 3:13. Christ hath redeemed us from the curse of the law. Rom. 5:18. By the righteousness of one, the free gift came upon all men unto justification of life. John 3:17. For God sent not his Son into the world to condemn the world; but that the world through him might be saved. 1 Tim. 4:10.

(*b*) Titus 2:11. For the grace of God, that bringeth salvation, hath appeared to all men. Rom. 5:20. But where sin abounded, grace did much more abound. Rom. 5:15.

(*c*) Joel 2:28. I will pour out my Spirit upon all flesh. John 16:8. And when he is come, he will reprove the world of sin. John 1:9. That was the true light, which lighteth every man that cometh into the world. Acts 2:17, 18. Job 32:8. Rev. 14:6.

all men,(*d*) and by these they receive power to repent and obey all the requirements of the gospel.(*e*) Hence it appears a perfect inconsistency to suppose that God would provide salvation for a less number than he really loved. As his love extended to all mankind, if he provided salvation for one, he must necessarily for all, there being nothing in his nature, nor in man's nature, whereby this provision should

---

(*d*) Prov. 8:4. Unto you, O men, I call; and my voice is to the sons of man. Isa. 45:22. Look unto me, and be ye saved, all the ends of the earth. Mark 16:15. Preach the gospel to every creature. Rom. 10:18. Have they not heard? Yes, verily, their sound went into all the earth, and their words unto the ends of the world. Rev. 22:17. Whosoever will, let him take the water of life freely. Matt. 24:14. Col. 1:23. Isa. 55:1.

(*e*) Phil. 1:29. Unto you it is given on the behalf of Christ—to believe on him. 1 John 5:3. His commandments are not grievous. If man has not received power to obey the gospel it follows that the commandments are grievous, and their author is unjust. Isa. 5:4. What could have been done more to my vineyard that I have not done in it? 1 Pet. 1:22. Ye have purified your souls in obeying the truth through the Spirit.

be limited.*(f)* The fact being admitted that God loves all men, that Christ died for all men, that the Holy Ghost reproves all men, that the gospel invites all men, and that, by virtue of these, all men have the ability to repent and believe, what other conclusion can be drawn than that the salvation of all is possible? We mean only to say, that salvation is *possible*, for though in its provision it is free and absolute,(*g*) yet in its application it is expressly conditional.(*h*) Salvation,

(*f*) Acts 10:34. God is no respecter of persons. Ezek. 18:25. Is not my way equal? 33:11. As I live, saith the Lord God, I have no pleasure in the death of the wicked: turn ye, turn ye, from your evil way. 2 Pet. 3:9. The Lord is not willing that any should perish, but that all should come to repentance. 1 Tim. 2:4. Who will have all men to be saved, and to come to the knowledge of the truth.

(*g*) John 3:16. God so loved the world, that he gave his only begotten Son, that whosoever believeth in him should not perish, but have everlasting life. Rom. 5:8. God commendeth his love towards us, in that while we were yet sinners, Christ died for us. 2 Cor. 5:14, 15.

(*h*) John 3:36. He that believeth on the

then, being freely provided, and ma being capable, through grace, of obtain ing it, if he perish, whom can he blam but himself? The charge must fal upon him with aggravated weight "*Thou hast destroyed thyself.*"

Son hath everlasting life; and he that be lieveth not the Son shall not see life.—Mark 16:16. John 3:24. Acts 13:39. 16:31

REMARKS. From these and other scrip tures, it is clear that God never designed tha the wicked should sin and die; but that in th plenitude of his mercy he has done all i his power, consistent with the moral govern ment of the world, for the salvation of men The sentiment that God is the author of sin and has decreed the wickedness of men, i derogatory to his character. The doctrin of universal decrees, however, has been argu ed from the foreknowledge of God; and fro this, many have inferred that the sinner can not repent. But that such arguments ar not conclusive, is evident from the followin reflections. 1. God's decrees cannot be th result of his foreknowledge, since an *infinite ly wise and good Being* can know of a futur event without decreeing that it shall come t pass. 2. If an event is *certain*, becaus God *knows* that it *will come to pass*, and a things occur of *necessity*, and the free agenc of man exists only in the imagination; i

CHAPTER VII.

Repentance.

The repentance which the gospel equires is a deep conviction, a pen-

---

ıust follow, on the same principle, that *God imself could not* have caused any event to ome to pass differently from what it has ıken place. All the arguments which seem ɔ prove that man is a subject of *necessity* are qually applicable to the Divine Being, and ave the same effect in relation to His gency. 3. The perfect knowledge of God, nstead of being the result of his decrees, s necessarily the result of his being *infinite* n his existence. Man knows but little, ecause with him the past is forgotten, the uture unknown, and he can exist in but ne place at the same time. God knows all hings, because he fills immensity, and because with him, one day is as a thousand years and a thousand years as one day. Consequently, foreknowledge, like *repentance* and *nger*, when applied to God, is a term adapted to *our* understanding, while strictly speaking with him there is no foreknowledge, for he fills all time and eternity, and with Him all is present. 4. God has *power* to make a moral agent, leaving him perfectly free to act in either of two ways, without any

itential sorrow, an open confession, decided hatred, and an entire forsakir of all sin.(*a*) This repentance Gc

---

circumstances that will compel his choice.- And having made man thus, the circur stance of the Infinite Existence beholdir the result of man's agency, could by I means destroy his *ability* to act *freely*. While God knows a sinner *will* sin, and *fina ly perish*, he knows at the same time, that h *can repent* and *live;* because he has given hi power so to do. Thus, when he sent Jer miah to the House of Judah, though he *kne* that they would not hear, he said, "*It ma be that the house of Judah will hear.*" Jer. 36: 37:2. And though he knew that the Israe ites would cause their children to pas through the fire unto Moloch, he sai "*Neither came it into my mind that they* SHOUL *do this abomination.*" Had he said, it came no into his mind that they WOULD do it, th conclusion would follow, that he did not *kno* of the event. But as he said, it came not int his mind that they *should* do this abomina tion, it follows that it was not *decreed;* for i is certain, that God could not have decree an event that never entered into his mind.

(*a*) Rom. 3:20. By the law is the knowl edge of sin. Rom. 7:9. When the command ment came, sin revived, and I died. 2 Co 7:10. For godly sorrow worketh repentanc to salvation not to be repented of. Ps. 51:17

is enjoined on all men, and without in this life the sinner must perish ernally.(*b*)

he sacrifices of God are a broken spirit: a oken and contrite heart, O God, thou wilt ot despise. Joel 2:12, 13. Therefore also ow, saith the Lord, turn ye even to me with l your heart, and with fasting, and with eeping, and with mourning; and rend your earts—and turn unto the Lord your God. rov. 28:13. He that covereth his sins, shall ot prosper: but whoso confesseth and forketh them shall have mercy. Ezek. 36:31. hen shall ye remember your own evil ways, nd your doings that were not good, and hall loathe yourselves in your own sight, for our iniquities, and for your abominations. Ezek. 14:6. Thus saith the Lord God, Reent and turn away your faces from all your bominations. Isa. 55:7: Let the wicked forake his way, and the unrighteous man his houghts; and let him return unto the Lord, nd he will have mercy upon him: and to our God, who will abundantly pardon. Ezek. 18: 0, 31. Repent, and turn yourselves from all our transgressions; so iniquity shall not be our ruin. Cast away from you all your ransgressions. Ps. 38:18. Hos. 5:15. John 12:25.

(*b*) Acts 17:30. But now [God] commandeth all men every where to repent. Mark 6:12. They went out and preached that men

CHAPTER VIII.

Faith.

True faith is an assent of the min to the great and fundamental truths c revelation;(*a*)an act of the understand ing in giving credit to the gospe through the influence of the Holy Spi

---

should repent. Acts 2:38. 3:19. Luke 13: But except ye repent, ye shall all likewis perish. John 9:4. The night cometh whe no man can work. 2 Thess. 1:7, 8, 9. Th Lord Jesus shall be revealed from heaven,— In flaming fire, taking vengeance on ther that know not God, and that obey not th gospel,—who shall be punished with ever lasting destruction. Acts 24:20. Matt. 4:17 11:20—22. 12:41. 21:31, 32.

(*a*) Heb. 11:6. He that cometh to Go must believe that he is, and that he is a re warder of them that diligently seek him.— John 5:46, 47. For had ye believed Moses, y would have believed me: for he wrote of me But if ye believe not his writings, how shal ye believe my words? Heb. 11:1: Faith i the substance of things hoped for, the evi dence of things not seen. John 16:27, 30 Ps. 119:66. Rom. 10:9.

t;(*b*) and a firm confidence and trust n the living God.(*c*) The fruit of faith s obedience to the gospel.(*d*) The power to believe is the gift of God;(*e*) but believing is an act of the creature, which is required as a condition of pardon, and without which the sinner cannot be regenerated, nor obtain salvation.(*f*) All men are required

(*b*) Rom. 10:10. With the heart man believeth unto righteousness. 1 Cor. 12:8, 9. For to one is given, by the Spirit, the word of wisdom;—to another, *faith*, by the same Spirit. Gal. 5:22. But the fruit of the Spirit is love—*faith*. Rom. 10:17.

(*c*) 2 Chron. 20:20. Believe in the Lord your God, so shall ye be established. Prov. 14:26. In the fear of the Lord is strong confidence. Rom. 4:20, 21. He staggered not at the promise of God through unbelief; but was strong in faith, giving glory to God: Being fully persuaded that what he had promised he was able also to perform. Eph. 3:12. 1 Tim. 4:10.

(*d*) James 2:17. Faith, if it hath not works, is dead, being alone. James 2:20—24, 26. Gal. 5:6. 1 Tim. 1:5.

(*e*) Phil. 1:29. Unto you it is given in the behalf of Christ,—to believe on him. Acts 14:27. 2 Pet. 1:1. Eph. 2:8.

(*f*) John. 6:29. This is the work of God,

to believe, and those who yield obedience to the obligation become the children of God by faith.(*g*)

---

that ye believe on him whom he hath sent. Mark 16:16. He that believeth—shall be saved. Acts 16:31. Believe on the Lord Jesus Christ, and thou shalt be saved. John 3:36. He that believeth on the Son hath everlasting life and he that believeth not the Son shall not see life; but the wrath of God abideth on him. John 8:21, 24. If ye believe not that I am he, ye shall die in your sins. Whither I go ye cannot come. Heb. 11:6. Without faith it is impossible to please him. Mark 1:15. Repent ye, and believe the gospel.

(*g*) Acts 10:43. Whosoever believeth in him shall receive the remission of sins. John 1:7. That all men through him might believe. Gal. 3:26. Ye are all the children of God by faith in Christ Jesus. Rom. 16:26. 5:1. John 3:15.

REMARKS. Some have said, that as man cannot believe without evidence, so he cannot disbelieve when sufficient evidence is presented. That this conclusion is incorrect, will appear from the following reasons. 1. Though the existence of God is demonstrated from the creation, and from the tender mercies which are over all his works, and, by the true light which lighteth every man; yet the most of the world remain in unbelief. 2. In

CHAPTER IX.

Regeneration.

As God is a holy Being and heaven a holy place, man must be regenerated before he can enter a state of happiness.(*a*) This change is an instantaneous renovation of the soul by the grace and Spirit of God,(*b*) whereby the penitent sinner receives new life,

---

every generation there have been multitudes, who, with the same testimony and the same evidences of the truth, have made opposite conclusions, and have taken different courses. 3. God condemns the sinner because he does not believe. This he would not do if he had not given him sufficient evidence and power to believe.

(*a*) Heb. 12:14. Follow—holiness, without which no man shall see the Lord. Rev. 21:27. And there shall in no wise enter into it any thing that defileth, neither whatsoever worketh abomination, or maketh a lie. Mat. 5:8. Gal. 5:19—21.

(*b*) John 3:5: Except a man be born of—the Spirit, he cannot enter into the kingdom of God. Ezek. 36:26, 27. A new heart will I give you, and a new spirit will I put within you; and I will take away the stony heart

becomes a child of God,(*c*) and is enabled to perform spiritual service.(*d*) It is called being born again, born of the Spirit,(*e*) being quickened,(*f*) passing from death unto life, (*g*) and a

---

out of your flesh, and I will give you a heart of flesh. And I will put my Spirit within you. Titus 3:5. Eph. 2:10.

(*c*) John 5:25. The hour is coming, and now is, when the dead shall hear the voice of the Son of God: and they that hear shall live. Eph. 2:10. For we are—created in Christ Jesus unto good works. 1 John 3:9. Rom. 8.16. The Spirit itself beareth witness with our spirit, that we are the children of God. John 1:12. James 1:18. 2 Cor. 5:17. Gal. 6:15.

(*d*) 1 Pet. 2:5. Ye also---are built up a spiritual house, an holy priesthood to offer up spiritual sacrifices. Ezek. 11:19, 20. Phil. 2:13. 1 Pet. 4:11.

(*e*) John 3:6. That which is born of the flesh is flesh; and that which is born of the Spirit is spirit. John 1:13. 3:5, 8. 1 John 3:9. 4 7, 5:1, 4:18.

(*f*) Eph. 2:1. And you hath he quickened, who were dead in—sins. Ps. 119:50, 93. Eph. 2:5. Col. 2:13.

(*g*) John 5:24. He that heareth my word, and believeth on him that sent me,—is passed from death unto life. 1 John 3:14.

partaking of the divine nature.(*h*)

CHAPTER X.

Justification and Sanctification.

Personal justification implies that the person justified has been guilty before God; and that, in consideration of the righteousness of Christ, received by faith, the sinner is pardoned and absolved from the guilt and punishment of sin.(*a*) Though the right-

(*h*) 2 Pet. 1:4. Whereby are given unto us exceeding great and precious promises; that by these ye might be partakers of the divine nature. Heb. 3:14.

(*a*) Rom. 5:16,17. The free gift is of many offences unto justification. For if by one man's offence death reigned by one; much more they which receive abundance of grace, and of the gift of righteousness, shall reign in life by one, Jesus Christ. Acts 13:39. And by him, all that believe are justified from all things, from which ye could not be justified by the law of Moses. Rom. 5:1,9. Therefore being justified by faith, we have peace

eousness of Christ is the foundation of the sinner's redemption, yet without repentance and faith it can never give him justification and peace with God.(*b*)

Sanctification is a work of God's grace, by which the soul is cleansed from all the pollutions of sin, and is

---

with God through our Lord Jesus Christ. Being now justified by his blood, we shall be saved from wrath through him. Isa. 53:11. Rom. 8:22—26.

(*b*) Acts 3.19. Repent ye, therefore, and be converted, that your sins may be blotted out. Heb. 4:2. But the word preached did not profit them, not being mixed with faith in them that heard it. Heb. 11:6. Without faith it is impossible to please him. Rom. 9:31, 32. Israel—hath not attained to the law of righteousness. Wherefore? Because they sought it not by faith. Rom. 3:25—30. Acts 13:38, 39.

REMARKS. That justification does not *precede* repentance and faith, and that these do not follow as *its fruits*, is evident from the following reasons: 1. When a man is *justified*, he is absolved from his sins, and the work of repentance must have been *already* accomplished. 2. Faith is required as a condition of salvation. "Believe in the Lord Jesus Christ and thou shalt be saved." 3. In Acts 3:19, repentance is required as a pre-

renewed after the image of God.(*c*) Though in regeneration the soul is sanctified, yet while the Christian continues in a state of trial, he has to contend with the corruptions of nature, and is liable again to be defiled.(*d*)

---

requisite to pardon or the remission of sins; and in John 3:18, the sinner is represented as being condemned, because he *has not* believed in Christ, and this is given as the reason why he cannot be justified. But if, on the other hand, repentance and faith are the *fruits* of justification, it follows, that regeneration is a sovereign act which is suddenly effected on the impenitent sinner, independently of his agency. This view of the subject seems to cast the blame on God, by representing that he neglects to effect the sovereign work of regeneration in sinners, which alone can produce repentance and faith, and yet condemns the sinner for not repenting and believing.

(*c*) 1 Cor. 6:11. And such were some of you; but ye are washed, but ye are sanctified, but ye are justified in the name of the Lord Jesus, and by the Spirit of our God. Heb. 10:10. By which will we are sanctified, through the offering of the body of Jesus Christ. John 17:17. Sanctify them through thy truth: thy word is truth. Col. 3:10. 2 Cor. 3:18. Eph. 5:26.

(*d*) Gal. 5:17. For the flesh lusteth against

Sanctification is also a setting apart the soul and body for holy service.(*e*) It is a progressive work, by which the Christian obtains victory over every temptation, corruption, and sinful inclination; and in which his will is brought into entire resignation to the will of God.(*f*) The attainment of entire sanctification in this life, is both the privilege and duty of every Christian.(*g*) For as sin is odious in the sight of God, Christ died to save his

---

the spirit. Rom. 8:13. If ye live after the flesh, ye shall die. Rom. 7:18—25.

(*e*) Ps. 4:3. The Lord hath set apart him that is godly for himself. Rom. 12:1. Present your bodies a living sacrifice, holy, acceptable unto God. See also Gen. 2:3. 1 Tim. 4:5.

(*f*) Heb. 6:1. Let us go on to perfection. 2 Pet. 3:18. But grow in grace. 1 John 5:4. This is the victory that overcometh the world, even our faith. Heb. 13:20,21. Now the God of peace—make you perfect in every good work to do his will. Col. 4:12. That ye may stand perfect and complete in all the will of God. Col. 1:9. Prov. 4:18. Eph. 6:12.

(*g*) 1 Thess. 5:23. And the very God of peace sanctify you wholly; and I pray God

people from it, and the gospel has sufficient power to complete the work during this probation. (*h*)

---

your whole spirit and soul and body be preserved blameless unto the coming of our Lord Jesus Christ. 1 Thess. 4:3. For this is the will of God even your sanctification. 2 Cor. 7:1. Having, therefore, these promises, dearly beloved, let us cleanse ourselves from all filthiness of the flesh and spirit, perfecting holiness in the fear of God. Gen. 17:1. Deut. 18:13. Col. 3:14.

(*h*) Eph. 5:25—27. Christ—loved the church, and gave himself for it; that he might sanctify and cleanse it, with the washing of water, by the word; that he might present it to himself a glorious church, not having spot, or wrinkle, or any such thing; but that it should be holy, and without blemish. 1 John 1:7, 9. And the blood of Jesus Christ his Son cleanseth us from all sin. If we confess our sins, he is faithful and just to forgive us our sins, and to cleanse us from all unrighteousness. Matt. 5:48. Be ye, therefore, perfect, even as your Father which is in heaven is perfect. 1 Pet. 1:16. Be ye holy; for I am holy. 1 John 5:3. And his commandments are not grievous. Col. 1:28. Whom we preach, warning every man, and teaching every man in all wisdom, that we may present every man perfect in Christ Jesus. Phil. 2:14, 15. Do all things without

CHAPTER XI.

Perseverance.

As the regenerate are placed in a state of trial during this life, their future obedience and final salvation are

---

murmurings and disputings; that ye may be blameless and harmless, the sons of God without rebuke, in the midst of a crooked and perverse nation, among whom ye shine as lights in the world. 2 Pet. 3:14. Be diligent that ye may be found of him in peace, without spot, and blameless. James 1:4. That ye may be perfect and entire, wanting nothing. John 1:47. Behold an Israelite indeed, in whom is no guile. 2 Cor. 13:11. Be perfect, be of good comfort. Phil. 3:15. 2 Tim. 3:17. Mat. 19:21. 1 John 2:5. 1 Pet. 5:10.

NOTE. The requirements and privileges of the scriptural doctrine of sanctification are exceedingly great. Though many doubt whether the Christian can become perfect in this life, yet this doctrine is clearly supported in the Holy Scriptures. We do not understand, however, that the Christian can become perfect in his *powers* and *faculties*, nor in the same sense that God is perfect; but that according to the ability which the Lord has given him, he can render *entire obedience*

ıeither determined nor certain. (*a*) It s, however, their duty and privilege

---

o his will, and become "filled with all the 'ulness of God."

(*a*) Ezek. 18:24. But when the righteous urneth away from his righteousness, and committeth iniquity, and doeth according to ıll the abominations that the wicked man do- ›th, shall he live? All his righteousness that ıe hath done shall not be mentioned: in his respass, that he hath trespassed, and in his sin that he hath sinned, in them shall he die. Ezek. 33:18. When the righteous turneth from his righteousness, and committeth in- iquity, he shall even die thereby. That this righteousness is not a "*self-righteousness*," or a "*hypocritical profession*," is inferred from the following reasons: 1. God declares that if the righteous man turns away from his right- eousness and committeth iniquity, he shall surely die. He would not have said this, had he alluded to *self-righteousness* or *hypocrisy*, unless he preferred such characters to those of honest men; for it could be no *crime* to turn away from self-righteousness and hy- pocrisy. 2. As death was the consequence of turning away from this righteousness, it is clearly inferred that life was the consequence of continuing in it. Therefore, it could not be self-righteousness, unless we admit that a man can be saved by self-righteousness. But Christ says, Except your righteousness shall

to be steadfast in the truth, to grow in

---

exceed the righteousness of the Scribes and Pharisees, ye shall in no case enter into the kingdom of heaven. John 15:6. If a man abide not in me, he is cast forth as a branch, and is withered. Heb. 6:4, 5, 6. For it is impossible for those who were once enlightened, and have tasted of the heavenly gift, and were made partakers of the Holy Ghost, and have tasted the good word of God, and the powers of the world to come, if they shall fall away, to renew them again unto repentance. 2 Pet. 2:20, 21. For if, after they have escaped the pollutions of the world, through the knowledge of the Lord and Savior Jesus Christ, they are again entangled therein, and overcome, the latter end is worse with them than the beginning. For it had been better for them not to have known the way of righteousness, than after they have known it, to turn from the holy commandment delivered unto them. Heb. 10:26. For if we sin wilfully after we have received the knowledge of the truth, there remaineth no more sacrifice for sins. 2 Pet. 1:10. If ye do these things, ye shall never fall. 1 Cor. 10:12. Let him that thinketh he standeth, take heed lest he fall. 2 Pet. 1:9. But he that lacketh these things is blind, and cannot see afar off, and hath forgotten that he was purged from his old sins. 1 Cor. 9:27. But I keep under my body, and bring it into subjection; lest that by any means, when I have preached to

grace, persevere in holiness, and make their election sure.(*b*)

---

others, I myself should be a castaway. 1 Tim 4:1. Now the Spirit speaketh expressly that in the latter times some shall depart from the faith, giving heed to seducing spirits, and doctrines of devils. Heb. 12:15. Looking diligently, lest any man fail of the grace of God. Heb. 4:1, 11. 12:15. 2 Pet. 3:14.

(*b*) 1 Cor. 15:58. Be ye steadfast, unmovable, always abounding in the work of the Lord. 2 Pet. 3:18. But grow in grace, and in the knowledge of our Lord and Savior Jesus Christ. Phil. 3:14. I press toward the mark, for the prize of the high calling of God in Christ Jesus. Mat. 24:13. But he that shall endure unto the end, the same shall be saved. Rom. 2:7. To them, who, by patient continuance in well doing, seek for glory, and honor, and immortality, eternal life. 1 Cor. 9:24. So run that ye may obtain. 2 Pet. 1:10, 11. Give diligence to make your calling and election sure; for if ye do these things, ye shall never fall. Rev. 2:7, 11, 17, 26. 3:5. 12:21. 21:7.

REMARKS.—Some have argued that the final perseverance of the saints is certain, because they are kept by the power of God through faith unto salvation. But if we reflect that this power is only used to keep the saints *through their faith*, and that some have put away faith and a good conscience, and

CHAPTER XII.

The Sabbath.

This is a seventh part of time, which from the creation of the world, God has set apart for a day of sacred rest and holy service. It was included in the ten commandments written on tables of stone, and given to Moses on Mount Sinai.(*a*) Nature itself teaches the necessity of its observance. Its

---

"*concerning faith made shipwreck,*" the argument loses all its apparent weight. Again, some have inferred that the final obedience of the regenerate is certain, because their souls are holy. But that this argument is not conclusive, appears evident from the fact that the Christian is no more holy than Adam was, who sinned while he was in the image of God.

(*a*) Gen. 2:3. And God blessed the seventh day and sanctified it. Ex. 20:8—10. Remember the Sabbath day to keep it holy. Six days shalt thou labor and do all thy work; but the seventh day is the Sabbath of the Lord thy God; in it thou shalt not do any work, thou, nor thy son, nor thy daughter, thy man-servant, nor thy maid-servant,

obligation is taught both in the Old and New Testaments, and is to continue with that of the other commandments till the end of time. As the law of the Sabbath was at first given to the whole world, it requires all men, on this day, to refrain from all servile labor, and devote themselves entirely to the service of the God that made them.(*b*)*

---

nor thy cattle, nor thy stranger that is within thy gates.

(*b*) Jer. 17:21. Thus saith the Lord, Take heed to yourselves, and bear no burden on the Sabbath day. Luke 23:56. And they rested on the Sabbath day according to the commandment. See also Isa. 58:13, 14. Ex. 16:23, 29. Mat. 5:19. Mark 10:19. 1 John 2:4. Mark 2:28. Therefore the Son of Man is Lord also of the Sabbath. Luke 24:1, 6. Acts 20:7. 1 Cor. 16:2. Rev. 1:9, 10.

---

* From the creation of the world, the seventh day of the week was observed as the Sabbath. But since the resurrection of Christ, the first day of the week has been kept instead of the seventh. It is inferred from the following, that this change was made by Christ or his apostles. 1. The seventh day was observed in remembrance of the work of creation, but as the work of

CHAPTER XIII.

The Church.

A Christian church is an assembly of persons who believe in Christ and worship the true God, agreeably to

---

redemption is creater than that of creation, it appears more suitable that the day on which it was completed by the resurrection of Christ should be observed in remembrance of this greater and more important event. 2. From the Scriptures, it is evident that the primitive Christians frequently assembled on the first day of the week for worship. 3. The history of the church shows that the first day of the week was universally kept as a day of rest and worship, instead of the seventh, from the days of the apostles. And this change appears to have been observed, with a very few exceptions, by the whole Christian world to the present day.

The Sabbath being a day of rest, it has been thought that previous to the coming of Christ, the seventh day was a figure of the rest which saints enjoy in this life; and that since the resurrection of the Son of God, the first day of the week points to that rest which remains for the redeemed. See Heb. 4:1-11.

his word.(*a*) In a more general sense, it signifies the whole body of real Christians throughout the world.(*b*) The church being the body of Christ,(*c*) none but the regenerate, who obey the gospel, are its real members.(*d*) Believers are received into a particular church, on their giving

(*a*) 1 Cor. 1:2. Unto the church of God which is at Corinth, to them that are sanctified in Christ Jesus, called to be saints. Acts 2:47. 2 Cor. 8:5. Rev. 2:1, 7, 8, 12, 18. 3: 1, 7, 14.

(*b*) Eph. 5:23. Christ is the head of the church. Eph. 1:22. 3:10. 5:25, 27. Gal. 1:18, 24.

(*c*) 1 Cor. 12:27. Now ye are the body of Christ. Col. 1:18.

(*d*) 1 Pet. 2:5. Ye also, as lively stones, are built up a spiritual house, a holy priesthood, to offer up spiritual sacrifices. 2 Cor. 6:14, 15. Be ye not unequally yoked together with unbelievers; for what fellowship hath righteousness with unrighteousness? and what communion hath light with darkness? And what concord hath Christ with Belial? or what part hath he that believeth with an infidel? John 18:36. My kingdom is not of this world. Gal. 4:28, 31. Rom. 9:8. Ps. 50:16. John 15:2, 6.

evidence of faith and being baptized.(*e*)

SECTION 1.—OFFICERS OF THE CHURCH.

The officers in the primitive church were apostles, bishops, and deacons.(*f*) The apostles were the especial *witnesses* of the works and sayings of Christ;(*g*) and of course this office ceased when their work was accomplished. The *gifts* perpetuated in the church are evangelists, pastors, teachers, helps, and governments.(*h*) These,

(*e*) Acts 2:41. Then they that gladly received his word were baptized; and the same day there were added unto them about three thousand souls. Gal. 3:27.

(*f*) Eph. 2:20. And are built upon the foundation of the apostles. Phil. 1:1. To the saints—which are at Philippi with the bishops and deacons. Luke 6:13. 1 Cor. 4:9.

(*g*) Acts 10:39. And we are witnesses of all things which he did. Acts 1:8. 5:32. Luke 24:48.

(*h*) Eph. 4:11. He gave some,—evangelists; and some, pastors and teachers. 1 Cor. 12:28. 2 Tim. 4:5. Acts 13:1.

however, do not appear to be distinct officers; but they imply different kinds of duties, which are performed by bishops or elders, deacons, and others.

1. *Bishops* are overseers,(*i*) who have the charge of souls—to instruct and rule them by the word.(*j*) They are called *elders*,(*k*) and they perform the duties of pastors, teachers, and evangelists.(*l*) The qualifications re-

(*i*) Acts 20:28. Take heed, therefore, unto yourselves, and to all the flock, over the which the Holy Ghost hath made you overseers. 1 Tim. 3:1—6.

(*j*) 1 Tim. 3:5. For if a man know not how to rule his own house, how shall he take care of the church of God? 1 Pet. 5:2. Feed the flock of God—taking the oversight thereof. Acts 20:28.

(*k*) Titus 1:5—7. Ordain elders in every city as I appointed thee: if any be blameless—for a *bishop* must be blameless. 1 Pet. 5:1. Acts 14:23. Compare Acts 20:28 with verse 17.

(*l*) 2 Tim. 4:5. But watch thou—do the work of an evangelist. Eph. 4:11, 12. 1 Tim. 3:2. "This officer is called a Pastor, Minister, Watchman, Elder, Teacher, Steward, and Ambassador, to represent the various

quired in a candidate for this office, are as follows:—He must be guiltless and the husband of but one wife. He must be watchful, prudent, and have the regular exercise of cool, dispassionate reason. His conduct and manners must be decent, orderly, and grave. He must be a lover of hospitality and

---

duties of his office. He is called Bishop, from the oversight he is to take; Pastor, from the spiritual food he is to administer; Minister, from the service he is to render; Watchman, from the vigilance he is to exercise; Elder, from the grave and prudent example he is to set; Teacher, from the instructions he is to give; Steward, from the mysteries or manifold grace he is to dispense; Ambassador, from the treaty of reconciliation and peace he is sent to effect." [Cogswell.] 1 Tim. 3:1. This is a true saying, If a man desire the office of a bishop, he desireth a good work. Jer. 3:15. And I will give you pastors according to mine heart, which shall feed you with knowledge and understanding. 1 Cor. 4:1. Let a man so account of us, as of the ministers of Christ, and stewards of the mysteries of God. Ezek. 3:17. Son of man, I have made thee a watchman unto the house of Israel. 1 Pet. 5:1. The elders which are among you I exhort, who am also an elder. Eph. 4:11. And he gave some—teachers. 2

of good men; ready to communicate, and able to teach.(*m*) He must be temperate; not quarrelsome; nor desirous of base gain. He must be meek; not contentious, neither a lover of money.(*n*) He must govern his family well; he must not be a young convert, but experienced in the things of God, and have a character not justly liable to reproach.(*o*) He must be

---

Cor. 5:20. Now, then, we are ambassadors for Christ, as though God did beseech you by us: we pray you in Christ's stead, be ye reconciled to God.

(*m*) 1 Tim. 3:2. A bishop then must be blameless, the husband of one wife, vigilant, sober, of good behavior, given to hospitality, apt to teach. Tit. 1:8. A lover of hospitality, a lover of good men, sober, just, holy, temperate. 2 Tim. 2:24, 25.

(*n*) 1 Tim. 3:3. Not given to wine, no striker, not greedy of filthy lucre; but patient, not a brawler, not covetous.

(*o*) 1 Tim. 3:4—7. One that ruleth well his own house, having his children in subjection with all gravity.—Not a novice, lest, being lifted up with pride, he fall into the condemnation of the devil. Moreover, he must have a good report of them which are without; lest he fall into reproach, and the snare of the devil. Titus 1:5—9. 2:7, 15.

especially called of God to the work;(*p*) adhere closely to the doctrine of Christ,(*q*) and be ordained by the laying on of hands.(*r*)

The duty of an elder or bishop is, 1. To be an ensample to the flock in

(*p*) Heb. 5:4. And no man taketh this honor unto himself, but he that is called of God, as was Aaron. Acts 20:28. Take heed—to all the flock over the which the *Holy Ghost* hath made you overseers. 1 Cor. 9:16. Necessity is laid upon me; yea, wo is unto me if I preach not the gospel. 2 Cor. 3:5, 6. 1 Tim. 1:12. Acts 13:2. Rom. 10:14, 15. 1 Cor. 9:17.

(*q*) Tit. 1:9. Holding fast the faithful word, as he hath been taught, that he may be able by sound doctrine, both to exhort and to convince the gainsayers. Tit. 2:1, 7, 8. But speak thou the things that become sound doctrine. In doctrine showing uncorruptness, gravity, sincerity, sound speech that cannot be condemned; that he that is of the contrary part may be ashamed, having no evil thing to say of you. 1 Tim. 1:3. 4:16. 2 Tim. 1:13. 1 Tim. 6:3, 4.

(*r*) 1 Tim. 4:14. Neglect not the gift that is in thee, which was given thee by prophecy, with the laying on of the hands of the presbytery. 1 Tim. 5:22. Lay hands suddenly on no man. Heb. 6:2. Acts 13:3.

all things.(*s*) 2. To examine into the spiritual state of all the souls under his care, and suit all his instructions, entreaties, and admonitions, to their condition. In this work is included the duty of a pastor.(*t*) 3. To study, preach the word, baptize, and administer the Lord's Supper.(*u*) 4. To do

(*s*) 1 Tim. 4:12. Be thou an example of the believers in word, in conversation, in charity, in spirit, in faith, in purity. 1 Pet. 5:3. Being ensamples to the flock. Tit. 2:7. In all things showing thyself a pattern of good works. Phil. 3:17.

(*t*) Heb. 13:17. For they watch for your souls, as they that must give account. 1 Pet. 5:2. Feed the flock of God,—taking the oversight thereof. 1 Tim. 4:6. If thou put the brethren in remembrance of these things, thou shalt be a good minister of Jesus Christ, nourished up in the words of faith and of good doctrine. Acts. 20:28. 2 Tim. 4:2. Jer. 3:15.

(*u*) 2 Tim. 2:15. Study to show thyself approved unto God, a workman that needeth not to be ashamed, rightly dividing the word of truth. 1 Tim. 4:15. Meditate upon these things; give thyself wholly to them; that thy profiting may appear to all men. 1 Tim. 4:13. Till I come, give attendance to reading, to exhortation, to doctrine. 2 Tim. 4:2.

according to his ability the work of an evangelist.(*v*) 5. As a steward he receives authority from Christ to rule the flock by the word. Therefore, he should neither act as a lord over God's heritage, nor yield to the doctrines and wickedness of men; but see that gospel discipline and holiness are enforced and practiced in the church.(*w*)

Preach the word; be instant in season, out of season: reprove, rebuke, exhort with all long suffering and doctrine. 2 Cor. 4:5. For we preach not ourselves, but Christ Jesus the Lord. Mat. 28:19. Teach all nations, baptizing them. Luke 22:19. Acts 20:11. 27:35.

(*v*) 2 Tim. 4:5. Do the work of an evangelist, make full proof of thy ministry. Mark 16:15. Go ye into all the world and preach the gospel to every creature. 2 Cor. 8:19. 10:15, 16. Acts 9:32. 15:41.

(*w*) Titus 1:7. For a bishop must be blameless, as the steward of God. 1 Pet. 5:3. Neither as being lords over God's heritage. Titus 2:15. These things speak, and exhort, and rebuke with all authority. 1 Tim. 1:3. I besought thee to abide—at Ephesus—that thou mightest charge some that they teach no other doctrine. 1 Tim. 4:16. Take heed unto thyself, and unto the doctrine; continue in them. 1 Tim. 4:11. These things com-

He should assist in ordaining elders and deacons, committing the things which he has learned of God to faithful men, who shall be able to teach others also. (*x*) The care and the salvation of souls being more important than every thing else, he should, as far as possible, avoid engaging in any temporal concerns which will divert his attention from his great calling, and devote himself wholly to the work. (*y*)

A *deacon* is a regular or stated servant of the church. As the bish-

---

mand and teach. 1 Tim. 5:17. Let the elders that rule well be counted worthy of double honor, especially they who labor in the word and doctrine. Tit. 1:5. Set in order the things that are wanting. Luke 22:25, 26. Heb. 13:7, 17, 24. 2 Tim. 2,14. 1 Tim. 4:6.

(*x*) Titus 1:5. That thou shouldest—ordain elders in every city. 2 Tim. 2:2. The same commit thou to faithful men, who shall be able to teach others also. Acts 6:3. 6.

(*y*) 2 Tim. 2:4. No man that warreth, entangleth himself with the affairs of this life, that he may please him who hath chosen him to be a soldier. 1 Tim. 4:15. Meditate upon these things; give thyself wholly to them;

ops were appointed to take the charge of souls, it is inferred that the seven appointed to minister to the saints (Acts 6:1—6) were *deacons*; and that as the former have the oversight of the spiritual concerns of the church, the latter have the charge of its temporal affairs, particularly in serving the tables of the needy.(*z*) Though there is no scriptural evidence that serving the *Lord's table* at communion was required of deacons, it appears that by common consent they have long performed this service in several denominations.

The *qualifications* required in a candidate for this office are the following. He must be sober, honest, temperate, not desirous of unrighteous gain, holding the mystery of the gospel in a pure

---

that thy profiting may appear to all. Acts 6:4. Isa 62:6. Ezek 3:17—21.

(*z*) Acts 6:1—4. When the number of the disciples was multiplied, there arose a murmuring—because their widows were neglected in the daily ministrations. Then the twelve—said, It is not reason that we should leave the word of God, and serve tables.

conscience. Being first proved he must be found blameless. His wife must also be serious, not a defamer, but sober and faithful in all things. He must have but one wife, and rule his children and his own house well.(*a*) He should be a wise man and filled with the Holy Spirit.(*b*) Having been selected by the church, he should be

---

Wherefore, brethren, look ye out among you, seven men of honest report—whom ye may appoint over this business. But we will give ourselves continually to prayer, and to the ministry of the word.

(*a*) 1 Tim. 3:8—12. Likewise must the deacons be grave, not double tongued, not given to much wine, not greedy of filthy lucre; Holding the mystery of the faith in a pure conscience. And let these also first be proved; then let them use the office of a deacon, being found blameless. Even so must their wives be grave, not slanderers; sober, faithful in all things. Let the deacons be the husbands of one wife, ruling their children and their own house well.

(*b*) Acts 6.3, 5. Look ye out among you seven men—full of the Holy Ghost and wisdom. And they chose Stephen, a man full of faith and the Holy Ghost.

appointed by prayer and the laying on of hands.(c)

Duties of a deacon. 1. He should attend to the temporal wants of the poor members of the church, that those called to labor in the gospel may give themselves to prayer and the ministry of the word. 2. As the design of his appointment was that the ministry might be freed from temporal care, the inference naturally follows that it is his duty to see that *their* wants also are supplied, lest they should be compelled to leave the word of God to serve their *own* tables. 3. There being no other officer in the church to superintend its *temporal affairs,* it is inferred from the nature of his office that the deacon should attend to all the concerns essential to its prosperity, which do not devolve on a bishop. 4. From the important nature of his qualifications, it has been considered his duty to take the lead of religious meetings in the absence of the minister.

(c) Acts 6:6. And when they had prayed, they laid their hands on them.

SECTION II.—ORDINANCES OF THE CHURCH.

The following ordinances or institutions were appointed by Christ or his apostles, and are obligatory on the church.

1. *Christian Baptism.*(*d*) This is the immersion of believers in water (*e*) in the name of the Father, Son, and

(*d*) Eph. 4:5. One Lord, one faith, one baptism. As true faith is inseparably connected with the *baptism of the Spirit*, and as water baptism was practiced in the primitive church under the influence of the Holy Ghost, Acts 10:5, 6, 44—47, it is manifest that the *one* baptism here spoken of alludes to an immersion in water.

(*e*) Col. 2:12. Buried with him in baptism. Rom. 6:4, 5. Buried with him by baptism. We have been planted together in the likeness of his death. Acts 8:38, 39. And they went down into the water, both Philip and the eunuch: and he baptized him. And, when they were come up out of the water, &c. Mat. 3:16. And Jesus, when he was baptized, went up straightway out of the water. John 3:23. And John also was baptizing in Enon, because there was much water there. Mark 1:5. And were all baptized of him in the river Jordan. Mat. 3:6. 1 Cor.

Holy Ghost,(*f*) in which are represented their death to the world, the washing of their souls from the pollu-

---

10:2. 15:29. Acts 16:13, 15, 32—34. Mr. Parkhurst, a Pædobaptist, defines the Greek verb *baptizo* from which *baptize* is derived,—"To *dip*, *immerse*, *plunge*." The history of the church shows that immersion was the *general practice* for 1300 years after the apostles. The Greek church, in whose language the New Testament was originally written, practice immersion invariably to this day. He that believeth and is baptized shall be saved. Mark 16:16. If thou believest with all thine heart thou mayest. Acts 8:37. Then they that gladly received his word were baptized. Acts 2:41. 16:33. Go teach (or disciple) all nations, baptizing them. Mat. 28: 19.

NOTE. That *believers* are the *only* subjects of baptism, is evident from the following considerations. 1. The commission of Christ does not authorize his ministers to baptize any others. 2. The New Testament gives no intimation that any others were baptized. 3. It is admitted by all to be a *sign of regeneration*, or the sanctifying influence of the Spirit, and it does not seem proper to affix a sign where there is no evidence that the thing signified does really exist.

(*f*) Mat. 28:19. 1 Cor. 1:13.

ions of sin,(*g*) their resurrection to newness of life, the burial and resurrection of Christ, their resurrection at the last day,(*h*) and their engagement to serve God.(*i*)

2. *The Lord's Supper* is designed to commemorate the sufferings of Christ, and to represent, in the use of bread and wine, the communion which saints have with him, and with each other.(*j*) Every *true believer* in

(*g*) Col. 3:3. Ye are dead, and your life is hid with Christ in God. Tit. 3:5. He saved us by the washing of regeneration. Heb. 10:22. Having—our bodies washed with pure water.

(*h*) Col. 2:12. Buried with him in baptism, wherein also ye are risen with him. Rom. 6:4. That like as Christ was raised up from the dead by the glory of the Father, even so we also should walk in newness of life. 1 Cor. 15:29. Else what shall they do which are baptized for the dead, if the dead rise not at all? why are they then baptized for the dead? Rom. 6:5.

(*i*) Gal. 3:27. As many of you as have been baptized into Christ, have put on Christ. Heb. 6:1,2.

(*j*) Mat. 26:26—28. Jesus took bread, and blessed it, and brake it, and gave it to the disciples, and said, Take, eat, this is my body

Christ being a member of his body, and a part of his visible church,* has not only a right to partake of his body and his blood in the communion, but

---

And he took the cup, and gave thanks, and gave it to them, saying, Drink ye all of it for this is my blood of the new testament which is shed for many for the remission of sins. Luke 22:19. This do in remembrance of me. 1 Cor. 11:23—26. For I have received of the Lord that which also I delivered unto you, That the Lord Jesus, the same night in which he was betrayed, took bread And, when he had given thanks, he brake it, and said, Take, eat; this is my body which is broken for you: This do in remembrance of me. After the same manner also he took the cup, when he had supped, saying, This cup is the new testament in my blood. This do ye, as oft as ye drink it, in remembrance of me. For as often as ye eat this bread, and drink this cup, ye do show the Lord's death till he come. 1 Cor. 10:16. The cup of blessing which we bless, is it not the communion of the blood of Christ? the bread which we

---

* It is the usual practice of our connexion, at the time of communion, to invite all Christians of good standing in any evangelical church, to partake with us; as, in general, such persons only are known as "true believers."

is under obligation thus to commemorate his death.(*k*)*

---

break, is it not the communion of the body of Christ? Luke 14:22—24.

(*k*) Eph. 1:22,23. And gave him to be the head over all things to the church, which is his body. 1 Cor. 10:17. For we, being many, are one bread and one body; for we are all partakers of that one bread. Col. 1:24. Acts 2:42. 20:7.

---

* *Washing the Saints' feet.* At our fifth General Conference, holden at Wilton, Me., in October, 1831, this subject was considered; and, after it had been harmoniously discussed, the following memorandum and agreement were made, viz. "Whereas the subject of washing the saints' feet has produced no small excitement among Christians of our denomination, some churches and individual members believing that they have sufficient evidence from the New Testament to warrant the practice as an ordinance of the gospel, while other churches and individual members have no evidence that satisfies their minds of its having been practised by the apostles:

"7. Agreed, therefore, that all persons in connection with us have a free and lawful right to wash feet or not, as may best answer their consciences to God; neither the performance or neglect of which should cause a breach of Christian fellowship."

3. *Public worship.* This is that service which the church or its members publicly render to God agreeably to his word.(*m*) Hearing the gospel signifies "listening, attending to, and obeying" the revealed will of God, as

---

(*m*) Heb. 10:25. Not forsaking the assembling of ourselves together—but exhorting one another. Acts 3:1. Now Peter and John went up together into the temple at the hour of prayer. Acts. 16:13. And on the Sabbath, we went out of the city by a river side, where prayer was wont to be made. 1 Thess. 5:11. Wherefore, comfort yourselves together, and edify one another, even as also ye do. Heb. 3:13. But exhort one another daily, while it is called to-day. 1 Cor. 14:31. For ye may all prophesy one by one, that all may learn, and all may be comforted. 1 Cor. 14:3,5. But he that prophesieth speaketh unto men to edification, and exhortation, and comfort. I would that ye all—prophesied. Acts 2:18. And on my servants, and on my hand-maidens, I will pour out in those days of my Spirit; and they shall prophesy. Phil. 4:6. In everything by prayer and supplication with thanksgiving, let your requests be made known unto God. Col. 3:16. Teaching and admonishing one another in psalms, and hymns, and spiritual songs, singing with grace in your hearts to the Lord. Eph. 4:11

contained in the Scriptures, and preached by his ministers.(*n*)

SECTION III.—DUTIES OF THE CHURCH.

The duty of the church is that obligation which the revelation of God enjoins upon it, collectively, or as individuals, for the manifestation of his manifold wisdom,(*o*) the perfection of

—14. Mat. 18:20. 1 Cor. 11:18,20. Acts 4:31. 11:26. 15:25. 12:5. Eph. 6:18. 1 Thess. 4:18. Rom. 12:6. Compare Acts 1:13, 14, with 2:1, 4. Luke 2:36—38. Eph. 5:19. Mark 14:26.

(*n*) Mat. 7:24. Whosoever heareth these sayings of mine and doeth them, I will liken him unto a wise man. 1 John 4:6. He that knoweth God, heareth us; he that is not of God, heareth not us. James 1:22. But be ye doers of the word, and not hearers only, deceiving your own selves. Mark 4:24. Take heed what ye hear:—and unto you that hear shall more be given. Rom. 10:14,17.—And how shall they hear without a preacher? So then, faith cometh by hearing, and hearing by the word of God. James 1:25. Rom. 2:13.

(*o*) Eph. 3:10, 11. To the intent that now unto the principalities and powers in heavenly places might be known, by the church, the manifold wisdom of God. According to the

the saints,(*p*) and the conversion of the world.(*q*) In this obligation are included the observance of the ten commandments,(*r*) entire obedience to the influences of the Spirit, (*s*) to the

---

eternal purpose which he purposed in Christ Jesus our Lord.

(*p*) Eph. 4:11—13. And he gave some, apostles; and some, prophets; and some, evangelists; and some, pastors and teachers; for the perfecting of the saints,—for the edifying of the body of Christ; till we all come in the unity of the faith, and of the knowledge of the Son of God unto a perfect man, unto the measure of the stature of the fulness of Christ.

(*q*) Mat. 5:16. Let your light so shine before men, that they may see your good works, and glorify your Father which is in heaven. Rom. 16:26. Mark 16:15. Mat. 5:13.

(*r*) Mat. 5:17, 19. Think not that I am come to destroy the law,—I am not come to destroy, but to fulfil. Whosoever, therefore, shall break one of these least commandments, and shall teach men so, he shall be called least in the kingdom of heaven. But whosoever shall do and teach them, the same shall be called great in the kingdom of heaven. Luke 23:56. And rested the Sabbath day according to the commandment. Mat. 22:37—40. Mark 10:19. Rom. 13:8—10.

(*s*) 1 Thess. 5:19. Quench not the Spirit.

institutions of the gospel, and to all the instructions and precepts of the Scriptures. (*t*)* Among the latter are the following particular requirements: Christian fellowship, (*u*) secret and family

Eph. 4:30. Grieve not the Holy Spirit. Rom. 8:1. There is—no condemnation to them which are in Christ Jesus, who walk not after the flesh, but after the Spirit. Gal. 5:16.

(*t*) John 5:3. For this is the love of God, that we keep his commandments: and his commandments are not grievous. Mat. 19:17.—But if thou wilt enter into life, keep the commandments. Mat. 5:48. Be ye, therefore, perfect, even as your Father which is in heaven is perfect. James 1:4—That ye may be perfect and entire, wanting nothing. 2 John 6. Isa. 8:20. 1 Cor. 7:19. John 14:21. Eccl. 12:13.

(*u*) 1 John 1:7. But if we walk in the light, as he is in the light, we have fellowship one with another. Acts 2:42. And they continued steadfastly in the apostles' doctrine and fellowship. Eph. 5:11. And have no fellow-

* The *ceremonial* and *typical* parts of the law of Moses pointed to the coming of Christ, and were fulfilled by him and abrogated when he nailed to his cross the hand-writing of ordinances that was against us. Of course, the ceremonial law, though instructive, is not now obligatory on the church.

prayer(*v*) domestic and social duties, (*w*)

---

ship with the unfruitful works of darkness, but rather reprove them. 1 John 1:3. Phil. 1:5.

(*v*) Mat 6:6. But thou when thou prayest, enter into thy closet; and when thou hast shut thy door, pray to thy Father which is in secret; and thy Father, which seeth in secret, will reward thee openly. Luke 6:12. Dan. 6:10. Acts 10:9. Jer. 10:25. Pour out thy fury upon the families that call not on thy name. Acts 10:2,30. A devout man, and one that feared God with all his house,—and prayed to God alway. And Cornelius said, Four days ago I was fasting until this hour; and at the ninth hour I prayed in my house. Ps. 55:17. Evening, and morning, and at noon will I pray, and cry aloud. The patriarchs and the masters of the families in Israel, built an *altar* wherever they cast a *tent;* how much more, then, should the heads of *Christian families* statedly maintain the worship of God in their *houses!* No man can well bring up his children in the fear and discipline of the Lord, without constantly reading the Scriptures, and praying in his family.

(*w*) Eph. 5:25. Husbands, love your wives, even as Christ also loved the church, and gave himself for it. Col. 3:19. Husbands, love your wives, and be not bitter against them. Eph. 5:28. So men ought to love their wives as their own bodies: he that loveth his wife loveth himself. Col. 3:18. Wives, submit

watchfulness, (x) administering to

---

yourselves unto your own husbands, as it is fit in the Lord. Eph. 5:24. As the church is subject unto Christ, so let the wives be to their own husbands in everything. 1 Pet. 3: 1. Eph. 6:4. Fathers, provoke not your children to wrath: but bring them up in the nurture and admonition of the Lord. Col. 3:21. Fathers, provoke not your children to anger lest they be discouraged. Gen. 18:19. I know him, that he will command his children and his household after him, and they shall keep the way of the Lord. Colossians 3:20. Children, obey your parents in all things; for this is well pleasing unto the Lord. Eph. 6:1, 2, 5, 9. Children, obey your parents in the Lord: for this is right. Honor thy father and mother. Servants, be obedient to your masters—in singleness of your heart, as unto Christ. And, ye masters, do the same things unto them, forbearing threatening, knowing that your Master also is in heaven: neither is there respect of persons with him. Col. 3: 22. Servants, obey in all things your masters:—not with eye service, as men-pleasers; but in singleness of heart, fearing God. Eph. 5:21. Submitting yourselves one to another in the fear of God. Rom. 12:10. Be kindly affectioned one to another with brotherly love: in honor preferring one another. Col. 3: 13. Forbearing one another, and forgiving

(x) See page 102.

the necessities of the poor and afflicted,(*y*) the support of those that

---

one another, if any man have a quarrel against any; even as Christ forgave you, so also do ye. Rom. 12:18. If it be possible, as much as lieth in you, live peaceably with all men. Mat. 5:44. Love your enemies, bless them that curse you, do good to them that hate you, and pray for them which despitefully use you, and persecute you. Mark 11:25, 26.—Forgive if ye have aught against any; that your Father also which is in heaven may forgive you your trespasses. But if ye do not forgive neither will your Father which is in heaven forgive your trespasses. Rom. 12:20. If thine enemy hunger, feed him; if he thirst, give him drink. Tit. 3:1. Put them in mind to be subject to principalities and powers, to obey magistrates, to be ready to every good work.

(*x*) Mark 13:37. What I say unto you, I say unto all, Watch. Mat. 26:41. Watch and pray, that ye enter not into temptation. 1 Cor. 16:13. Watch ye, stand fast in the faith, quit you like men, be strong. 1 Pet. 4:7. Be ye therefore sober and watch unto prayer. 1 Pet. 5:8. Be sober, be vigilant; because your adversary the devil, as a roaring lion, walketh about, seeking whom he may devour.

(*y*) Luke 18:22. Sell all thou hast, and distribute unto the poor, and thou shalt have treasure in heaven. Mat. 19:21. Prov. 28:27. He that giveth unto the poor shall not lack. Prov. 19:17. He that hath pity upon the poor

preach the gospel, (z) and the

---

lendeth unto the Lord; and that which he hath given will he pay him again. Luke 11: 41. But rather give alms of such things as ye have. Luke 12:33. Sell that ye have, and give alms. Deut. 15:7, 11. Thou shalt not—shut thine hand from thy poor brother. For the poor shall never cease out of the land; therefore I command thee, saying, Thou shalt open thine hand wide unto thy brother, to thy poor, and to thy needy, in thy land. John 12:6. Rom. 15:26. Gal. 2:10. 1 Cor. 16:1, 2. James 1:27. Pure religion and undefiled before God and the Father, is this, to visit the fatherless and widows in their afflictions, &c. Mat. 25:36. Naked and ye clothed me; I was sick, and ye visited me; I was in prison, and ye came unto me. 1 Tim. 5:10. If she have relieved the afflicted. Acts 6:1. Phil. 4: 14.

(z) Mat. 10:9, 10. Provide neither gold, nor silver, nor brass in your purses: Nor scrip for your journey, neither two coats, neither shoes, nor yet staves: for the workman is worthy of his meat. Luke 10:7. For the laborer is worthy of his hire. 1 Cor. 9:4, 6, 11, 13, 14. Have we not power to eat and to drink? Have we not power to forbear working? Who goeth a warfare at any time at his own charges? who planteth a vineyard, and eateth not of the fruit thereof? or who feedeth a flock, and eateth not of the milk of the flock? Say I these things as a man? or saith not the law the same also? For it is

exercise of church discipline.(*a*)

---

written in the law of Moses, Thou shalt not muzzle the mouth of the ox that treadeth out the corn. For our sakes, no doubt this is written. If we have sown unto you spiritual things, is it a great thing if we shall reap your carnal things? Do ye not know that they which minister about holy things live of the things of the temple? and they which wait at the altar are partakers with the altar? Even so hath the Lord ordained, that they which preach the gospel should live of the gospel. Gal. 6:6. Let him that is taught in the word, communicate unto him that teacheth in all good things. 2 Cor. 11:8, 9. I robbed other churches, taking wages of them to do you service. For that which was lacking to me the brethren which came from Macedonia supplied. Deut. 12:19. Phil. 4:16, 18.

(*a*) Mat. 18:15—17. Moreover, if thy brother shall trespass against thee, go and tell him his fault between thee and him alone: if he shall hear thee, thou hast gained thy brother. But if he will not hear thee, then take with thee one or two more, that in the mouth of two or three witnesses every word may be established. And if he shall neglect to hear them, tell it unto the church: but if he neglect to hear the church, let him be unto thee as a heathen man and a publican. 1 Tim. 5:20. Them that sin rebuke before all. Gal. 6:1. Brethren, if a man be overtaken in a fault,

CHAPTER XIV.

Death.

The bodies of men being subject to the calamities of the fall, all have died,

---

ye which are spiritual, restore such a one in the spirit of meekness. 2 Thess. 3:6. Now we command you, brethren, in the name of our Lord Jesus Christ, that ye withdraw yourselves from every brother that walketh disorderly, and not after the tradition which ye received of us. James 5:16. Confess your faults one to another, and pray one for another. 1 Cor. 5:11, 13. But now I have written unto you not to keep company, if any man that is called a brother be a fornicator, or covetous, or an idolater, or a railer, or a drunkard, or an extortioner; with such an one no not to eat. Therefore put away from among yourselves that wicked person. Rom. 16:17. Mark them which cause divisions and offences, contrary to the doctrine which ye have learned; and avoid them. 2 John 10. If there come any unto you and bring not this doctrine, receive him not into your house, neither bid him God speed. Titus 3:10. A man that is a heretic, after the first and second admonition, reject. 1 Tim. 5:19. Against an elder receive not an accusation, but before two or

or will die, excepting Enoch, Elijah, and the saints that shall be on the earth at the last day.(*a*) But the soul, spirit, or the immaterial part, survives the dissolution of the body, and immediately after death enters a state of happiness or misery.(*b*)

---

three witnesses. 2 Cor. 2:6, 7, 8. 1 Cor. 5: 4, 5. 1 Tim. 1:20. 6:3—5.

(*a*) Rom. 5:12. By one man, sin entered into the world, and death by sin; and so death passed upon all men. Heb. 9:27. It is appointed unto men once to die. Heb. 11: 5. Enoch was translated that he should not see death. 2 Kings 2:11. There appeared a chariot of fire and horses of fire,—and Elijah went up by a whirlwind into heaven. 1 Thess. 4:17. Then we which are alive and remain, shall be caught up together with them in the clouds, to meet the Lord in the air. 1 Cor. 15:52. Ps. 89:48. Eccl. 8:8.

(*b*) Eccl. 12:7. Then shall the dust return to the earth as it was; and the spirit shall return unto God who gave it. Luke 23:43. And Jesus said unto him, Verily I say unto thee, To-day shalt thou be with me in paradise. Phil. 1:23. Having a desire to depart, and to be with Christ, which is far better.—Mat. 17:3. And behold, there appeared unto them Moses and Elias, talking with him. Mat. 22:31, 32. Have ye not read that—I am

CHAPTER XV.

The Resurrection.

As the transgression of Adam secured temporal death to all his posterity, so the obedience and resurrection of Jesus Christ render it certain that the bodies of all men will be raised from

---

the God of Abraham, and the God of Isaac, and the God of Jacob? God is not the God of the dead, but of the living. Acts 7:59. And they stoned Stephen, calling upon God, and saying, Lord Jesus, receive my spirit. Rev. 6:9. I saw under the altar, the souls of them that were slain for the word of God, and for the testimony which they held. Mat. 10:28. Fear not them which kill the body, but are not able to kill the soul. 2 Cor. 5:8. We are —willing rather to be absent from the body, and to be present with the Lord. Luke 16: 22, 23, 24. The beggar died, and was carried by the angels into Abraham's bosom: the rich man also died, and was buried; and in hell he lifted up his eyes, being in torments, and seeth Abraham afar off, and Lazarus in his bosom And he cried, and said, Father Abraham, have mercy on me; and send Lazarus, that he may dip the tip of his finger in

the dead(*a*). The doctrine of the res

---

water and cool my tongue; for I am torment ed in this flame. Jude 7. Sodom and Go morrah—are set forth for an example, suffer ing the vengeance of eternal fire.

(*a*) 1 Cor. 15:21, 22. For since by mai came death, by man came also the resurrec tion of the dead. For as in Adam all die even so in Christ shall all be made alive. 1 Cor. 15:13—19. But if there be no resurrec tion of the dead, then is Christ not risen And if Christ be not risen, then is our preach ing vain, and your faith is also vain. Yea and we are found false witnesses of God; be cause we have testified of God, that he raised up Christ; whom he raised not up, if so be that the dead rise not. For if the dead rise not, then is not Christ raised; and if Christ be not raised, your faith is vain; ye are yet in your sins. Then they also which are fall en asleep in Christ are perished. If in this life only we have hope in Christ, we are of all men most miserable. Acts 24:15. There shall be a resurrection of the dead, both of the just and unjust. Job 19:25, 26. For I know that my Redeemer liveth, and that he shall stand at the latter day upon the earth: And though, after my skin, worms destroy this body, yet in my flesh shall I see God. Isa. 26:19. Thy dead men shall live, together with my dead body shall they arise. Mat. 22: 30. Acts 26:8. John 5:28, 29. 2 Tim. 2:18. Acts 26:8. Rom. 8:11.

rrection is not only taught in the Scriptures, but it is intimated in the atural world.(*b*) The saints will be aised in the likeness of Christ; but ie wicked will awake unto shame and verlasting contempt.(*c*)

(*b*) Job 14:7, 14, 15. For there is hope of a 'ee, if it be cut down, that it will sprout again nd that the tender branches thereof will not ease. If a man die shall he live again? All ie days of my appointed time will I wait, ll my change come. Thou shalt call, and I ill answer thee: thou wilt have a desire to ie work of thine hands. 1 Cor. 15:36. That hich thou sowest is not quickened, except die.

(*c*) Phil. 3:21. Who shall change our vile ody, that it may be fashioned like unto his lorious body. 1 Cor. 15:53. For this orruptible must put on incorruption, and iis mortal must put on immortality. 1 ohn 3:2. But we know, that, when he shall ppear, we shall be like him. Ps. 17:15. shall be satisfied, when I awake with thy likeess. Dan. 12:2. And many of them that eep in the dust of the earth shall awake, ome to everlasting life, and some to shame nd everlasting contempt. John 5:28, 29. 'he hour is coming, in the which all that are i the grave shall hear his voice, and shall ome forth; they that have done good unto ie resurrection of life; and they that have

CHAPTER XVI.

The General Judgment.

As men do not receive the due re ward of all their deeds in this life,* there will be a general judgment, wher time and man's probation will close for·

done evil unto the resurrection of damnation Mat. 25:32—46.

* That the impenitent are not punished ir this life according to their sins is manifes from the following considerations. 1. Wher a person commits suicide in such a manne that life is closed without affording any tim for repentance, or when one dies in a state o intoxication, it is impossible that he shoul have been punished for his last crime, sinc no just government can punish a sin before i is committed. 2. All men have not comple-ted the work of their iniquity at the time o their dissolution. But their examples, anc their writings, like those of Paine and Vol-taire, still remain to fill up the cup of thei iniquity. 3. Such is the magnitude of the sinner's transgressions, that the punishments of this life are not adequate to his great guilt 4 Punishment in this life is neither equal nor proportionate to crime, because those

ever.(*a*) Then all men will be judged according to their works:(*b*) the

---

who are the most wicked do not receive the most punishment. The wicked often flourish "like the green bay tree"—"they are not in trouble as other men," and to one it was said, "Thou in thy life time receivedst thy good things." 5. The doctrine of future rewards and punishments is expressly taught in the Holy Scriptures, as will appear from the following quotations.

(*a*) Acts 17:31. Because he hath appointed a day in which he will judge the world in righteousness by that man whom he hath ordained. 2 Pet. 2:9. The Lord knoweth how —to reserve the unjust unto the day of judgment to be punished. Mat. 11:24. It shall be more tolerable for the land of Sodom in the day of judgment, than for thee. 2 Pet. 3:7. But the heavens and the earth, which are now, by the same word are kept in store, reserved unto fire, against the day of judgment and perdition of ungodly men. Jude 6. And the angels which kept not their first estate—he hath reserved in everlasting chains under darkness, unto the judgment of the great day. Rev. 10:6. There should be time no longer. 1 Cor. 15:24. Then cometh the end, when he shall have delivered up the kingdom to God, even the Father. Mat 12:41. 42. 25:31, 32. 1 John 4:17. 2 Pet. 3:11, 12. Rev. 20:11, 12

(*b*) 2 Cor. 5:10. For we must all appear

righteous will enter into eternal life,(*c*)

---

before the judgment seat of Christ: that every one may receive the things done in his body, according to that he hath done, whether it be good or bad. Rom. 2:16. In the day when God shall judge the secrets of men, by Jesus Christ, according to my gospel. Eccl. 11:9. For all these things God will bring thee into judgment. Eccl. 12:4. For God shall bring every work into judgment, with every secret thing, whether it be good, or whether it be evil. Mat. 12:36. Every idle word that men shall speak, they shall give account thereof in the day of judgment. Rev. 20:13. And the sea gave up the dead which were in it; and death and hell delivered up the dead which were in them: and they were judged every man according to their works. Rom. 2:6. Who will render to every man according to his deeds. Rom. 2:7—9. 14:10, 12. Eccl. 3: 17.

(*c*) Mat. 25:34, 46. Then shall the King say unto them on his right hand, Come, ye blessed of my Father, inherit the kingdom prepared for you from the foundation of the world. The righteous [shall go] into life eternal. 2 Pet. 1:11. For so an entrance shall be ministered unto you abundantly, into the everlasting kingdom of our Lord and Savior Jesus Christ. Rev. 3:12. Him that overcometh will I make a pillar in the temple of my God. 1 Thess. 4:17. So shall we ever be

and the wicked will go into a state of endless punishment.(*d*)

---

with the Lord. Rom. 6:22. Rev. 1:6. 3:4. Col. 3:4.

(*d*) Mat. 25:41, 46. Then shall he say also unto them on the left hand, Depart from me, ye cursed, into everlasting fire, prepared for the devil and his angels. And these shall go away into everlasting punishment. 2 Thess. 1:9. Who shall be punished with everlasting destruction from the presence of the Lord. Mark 3:29. But he that shall blaspheme against the Holy Ghost hath never forgiveness, but is in danger of eternal damnation. Mark 9:44. Their worm dieth not, and the fire is not quenched. Jude 7. Even as Sodom and Gomorrah,—are set forth for an example, suffering the vengeance of eternal fire.—Rev. 14:11. And the smoke of their torment ascendeth up for ever and ever. John 8:21. Rev. 20:10, 15. 21:8, 27. 22:11. Mat. 13:41, 42. Ps. 9:17. 11:6.

REMARKS. That the soul of man is immortal and will exist eternally is evident from the following propositions. 1. It was originally made in the *image of God*, and was called a *living soul*. 2. It has the control of the body, and can exist independently from the body. 3. It possesses boundless capacities and desires, which cannot be filled with the things of this life. 4. It is capable of thinking, has a sense of right and wrong, feels the stings of guilt, and has a consciousness of the providence and justice of God.—5. As it is immaterial, it is not subject to corruption, consequently it is imperishable. 6. The Scriptures teach the doctrine of eternal rewards and punishments, and, of course, the soul must exist forever and ever. See the preceding quotations.

USAGES

OF THE

FREE-WILL BAPTIST CONNEXION,

REVISED

BY ORDER OF THE

THIRTEENTH GENERAL CONFERENCE,

ASSEMBLED IN OCT., 1847.

PREFACE TO THE REVISED EDITION.

At the Thirteenth Session of the General Conference of the Free-will Baptists of North America, held in Sutton, Vt., in Oct., 1847, a committee was appointed to revise the published usages of the denomination. Said committee reported a draft for a revised edition of those usages, which was accepted by the General Conference, and referred to another committee for farther revisal and preparation for the press. This committee have attended to the duty assigned them, and submit the following, which they believe to be a fair exposition of the practices which prevail at the present time in the denomination. It will be perceived that no alteration has taken place in the principles, doctrine or polity of the denomination, since the publication of the previous edition. Since that event, however, their usages have become more thoroughly systematized, as has been evinced from time to time in the acts of the various sessions of the General Conference, to which the committee have had a special reference in preparing this work. In its present form this work is designed to be not only an exponent of the practices of our beloved connexion to those who are not personally acquainted with them, but also a convenient text book for the church member, and a manual for the Clerks of churches, Q. M's and Y. M's.

It is confidently believed that the Confession of Faith, which may be found in the sixth chapter, is as good an embodiment of Scripture doctrine as can be found in the same compass in the English language or any other, and will be found, together with the Covenant, a great convenience in organizing churches: and would all the churches throughout the connexion adopt them, and thus secure a uniformity in the principles of their organization, we believe it would greatly tend to the glory of God, and become, to the various branches of our denomination, the medium through which they should see eye to eye. The committee also believe that the "forms" and tables, which have been prepared at no small expense of time and labor, will prove an almost invaluable aid to all who may consult them. Should these forms be carefully consulted by Clerks, an incalculable amount of perplexity would be saved, from year to year, which now occurs in relation to our statistics. And should the work be thoroughly studied by ministers and church members, we confidently believe it would be found to contain plain, practical hints, which would furnish a solution to many a difficult question in church labor.

A perfect uniformity of practice, of course, does not prevail in all our churches—therefore the committee have been sometimes under the necessity of choosing, among different customs, the one which they deem most advisable, keeping in mind an action of the last session of the General Conference, which is as follows:

"*Resolved*, That the usages which have just been adopted, are not published as the invariable rule of every church, neither as a code of laws, but as showing the prevailing practice of the denomination, which we hereby commend to all the churches." COMMITTEE OF REVISION.

June 14, 1848.

PREFACE TO THE FIRST EDITION.

It seems impossible for any lawgiver, however wise, to make all the regulations, which, in the mutability of human affairs, are necessary for his subject. General principles are all that can be unalterably fixed. Hence some things are necessarily left for particular communities to regulate according to their peculiar circumstances. It is, however, required of such communities that their regulations be in perfect accordance with the general laws under which they act. Our national government could not well regulate all the internal concerns of the States, nor the individual States wisely direct all the affairs of the different towns. Neither do the Scriptures profess to give all the particular rules which may be necessary to all parts of the church in the different places and ages of the world. Many examples might be brought from the Scriptures to demonstrate the truth of this proposition, but two or three may suffice. Our Lord broke the bread and poured the cup, and commanded his disciples to do the same. But had a rule been given requiring the precept to be practiced on particular days, and at stated times, local circumstances in many instances would have rendered obedience inconvenient or impracticable. The Scripture saith, "Forsake not the assembling of yourselves together." But had a command been given, showing how often a church should come together, it could not have been well adapted to all congregations, times and seasons. Christ instituted the visible church, and the apostles planted churches; members were received and excluded, but no rule is given as to the particular method used in their reception or rejection.

Hence, though the church has a perfect law in relation to the doctrine of Christ, and the general principles of practice, it is manifestly the duty of every religious community to make such local and temporary regulations as, in their peculiar circumstances, are necessary to secure obedience to the perfect law by which they are to be governed. In relation to the kind of obligation just named, the apostle inquires of the church at Corinth,—"Doth not even nature itself teach you?" 1 Cor. 11:14.—And Christ says, "Yea, and why even of yourselves judge ye not what is right?" Luke 12:57. Again, Paul says to the church at Corinth, "Do ye not know that the saints shall judge the world, and if the world shall be judged by you, are ye unworthy to judge the smallest matters?" 1 Cor. 6:2. And Peter, speaking to the saints in general, says, "Yea, all of you be subject one to another." 1 Pet. 5:5.

USAGES, ETC.

CHAPTER I.

THE CHURCH.

SECTION I. ORGANIZATION.

When several believers wish to become a church in connection with the F. W. Baptist denomination, they send a request to a Quarterly Meeting for a council; or they select a council themselves, consisting of ministers, or ministers and laymen. The council, on meeting them, proceed in the following manner, viz.:

1. After prayer the council organize by choosing a chairman and secretary.

2 The council then ascertain the number of individuals, who desire to be organized into a church, receive and read their letters of dismission from

other churches, or obtain the evidence of their Christian character and eligibility to church membership.

It is then ascertained that perfect Christian fellowship exists among them all.

3. The council read the doctrinal views of the F. W. Baptists, which are contained in the Treatise on their Faith,* and ascertain that all the candidates agree with those sentiments.

4. A Covenant is then read and adopted by the candidates.

5. Inquiry is then made in relation to their ability and prospects for sustaining regular preaching. If this examination prove satisfactory to the council, and if in their opinion it would be for the glory of God to organize them into a church, the council proceed to the organization as follows:

(1.) The candidates arise and join their hands together.

---

* If considered preferable, for the sake of brevity, the "Confession of Faith" may be read, which may be found in Chap. 6, Sect. 1, of this work.

(2.) One of the council gives them the hand of fellowship in behalf of the council, and acknowledges them as a Christian church, organized according to the usages of the Free-will Baptist denomination.

(3.) A consecrating prayer is then offered and followed by a song of praise to God.

(4.) The church then proceed (the chairman of the council presiding) to make choice of a standing clerk, whose duty it is to keep a book of records, containing the names of all the members and all the votes of the church. A pastor is also elected, who presides as moderator in the meetings of the church.*

Generally on these occasions a sermon is preached, or an address is given to the church by one of the council. When a pastor is chosen at the organ-

---

* When it is not convenient for a church to elect a pastor at its organization, or when the office of pastor becomes vacant in any church, a member of the church is selected for moderator till a pastor is obtained.

ization, some services appropriate to the recognition of that important relation are performed by the council.*

SECTION II. OFFICERS OF THE CHURCH.

The regular officers of a Free-will Baptist church are a pastor, two or more deacons, a clerk and treasurer. A standing committee, or committee of discipline for the prosecution of labors in the church, and an examining committee to examine candidates for membership, and to make inquiries relative to their characters, are also chosen in some churches.

The pastor, clerk and deacons usually hold their offices till they are dis-

---

* NOTE 1. It is contrary to the usage of the denomination for ministers to assist in the organization of a church composed of disaffected members, within the limits of another church which is in good standing in the denomination.

NOTE 2. When individuals are so situated that it is inconvenient for them to enjoy ordinary church privileges, they become connected with some church as a branch, maintaining separate prayer, conference meetings, &c

nissed by the church or removed by leath.

SECTION III. GOVERNMENT OF THE CHURCH.

Every Free-will Baptist church s an independent body so far as it relates to its own government, the transaction of its own business, the choice of its officers, and the discipline of its members.

SECTION IV. ON RECEIVING AND DISMISSING MEMBERS.

All persons who become members of the church are received by a unanimous vote. On making a profession of religion, the candidate is required to give satisfactory evidence of having experienced a change of heart by the Spirit of God; and must receive the ordinance of baptism. Persons who are members of other evangelical churches, and who have been baptized, are received by vote, on presenting a letter of commendation from the churches to which they belong.

The hand of fellowship is given to all who join the church by the pastor, or by some ordained minister of the denomination, when the church has no pastor.

2. It is contrary to F. W. Baptist usages for any church to receive an individual who has been expelled from a sister church, unless satisfaction shall first be made to the church from which such individual has been expelled.

3. It is also considered improper to receive a member who has been expelled from a church of any other evangelical denomination, until suitable reparation has been made by such member.

4. When a member in good standing removes from the limits of the church to which he belongs, or wishes to unite with another evangelical denomination, he applies to the church for a letter of commendation, which is given by a vote of the church. When said church is duly notified of his connection with another church, he is no longer considered a member of the for-

mer. This notice is given by the clerk of the church with which said member unites.*

SECTION V. MEETINGS OF THE CHURCH.

1. Every well regulated church has a pastor and maintains the public worship of God on the Sabbath.

2. A regular monthly conference is usually established in each church, at which the several members, when practicable, are expected to be present and speak to each other of their religious exercises, and renew their covenant with God and each other.

3. A church meeting for the transaction of business is appointed to be holden at such stated times as the church may deem advisable. Special meetings are held as occasion requires.

4. In many churches classes are or-

---

*Note. It is considered contrary to our usages for members to receive letters of dismission or commendation unless they intend to connect themselves with another evangelical church.

ganized, composed of church members and others, and led by such brethren as have been appointed by the church or chosen by the class for the purpose. These meetings are usually held weekly, and are free for any person to attend. All members present are requested to give an account of their religious enjoyment, &c., anxious persons are conversed with by the class-leader and prayed for. These classes are usually reported at the church meeting by the class-leaders.

5. A meeting for prayer and conference is generally held in each church, once a week or oftener, in which any Christian or any inquirer for salvation has liberty to speak or pray.

6. The church usually partake of the Lord's Supper once in two months, or oftener.*

---

* NOTE. The following vote was passed by the General Conference in 1847, viz.:

"It is earnestly recommended by the Thirteenth General Conference of the Free-will Baptists that the churches of our denomination celebrate the Lord's Supper once a month where it is practicable."

SECTION VI. CONNECTION OF THE CHURCH WITH THE QUARTERLY MEETING.

1. Every church in order to be connected with the Free-will Baptist denomination must become a member of some Q. M. in the denomination. The objects for which churches unite together in a Q. M. are union, strength and mutual aid, that they may thereby be better prepared to glorify God, advance truth, and benefit the world.

2. A church becomes a member of a Q. M. by presenting a written application for membership and receiving a vote of the Q. M.

3. The church elects delegates to attend each session of the Q. M., and reports its religious state by letter, as required by the Constitution of the Q. M. to which the church belongs. The report containing the annual statistics is made to the first session of the Q. M. after the first Sabbath in April. See form of Report, Chap. VI. Sec. V. Art. 7.

Section VII. The Ministry.

1. The pastor of each church is expected to become a member of the church of which he is pastor, unless he should have the pastoral charge of more than one church at the same time, in which case he should be a member of one of those churches.

2. When a church obtains an evidence that one of their members is called of the Lord to preach the gospel, they request the Q. M. to examine him in relation to his piety, qualifications, call to the ministry, and, if they judge expedient, to give him a license to preach.

3. A church desiring the ordination of one of their members who has been previously licensed, either request the Q. M. to send them a council or select one themselves. The council, on gaining evidence that his qualifications are such as the Scriptures require for the work of the ministry, ordain him by the imposition of hands with prayer, giving him a charge and the right hand of fellowship.

4. When a minister of another denomination wishes to unite with the Free-will Baptists, he makes his request to a church. If the church on examination are satisfied, they call a council of ministers to sit with them for further examination; and if he is approved by the council, he is admitted as a member of the church.*

5. When a minister in good standing makes a request for a letter to unite with another denomination, the church call a council of ministers, who in the presence of the church, inquire into the reasons for his request; and in case he still urges it, and his Christian character is good and his doctrine is not heretical, the church give him a letter of dismission.

6. It is the duty of every church that engages the services of a preacher, to give him seasonable and suitable compensation.

---

* In such cases, if the minister has been regularly ordained by an evangelical denomination, usually his ordination is considered valid by Free-will Baptists.

7. No minister is considered a member of the denomination unless he is a member of some church.

SECTION VIII. DISCIPLINE OF THE CHURCH.

1. In all cases of private offence, that is, when one member is grieved with another on account of some unchristian conduct which is not publicly known, it is the duty of the aggrieved party to pursue the directions given by our Lord in Mat. 18:15, &c.

2. When a member commits a public transgression—openly reproaches the cause of religion—violates his covenant obligations, or when there are reports publicly circulated unfavorable to the Christian character of any member, the church, to which such member belongs, through a committee or otherwise, immediately calls the offender to an account,—examines the nature of the offence, or inquires into the character of the report, and if such member on being found guilty does not give satisfactory evidence of true pen-

itence, after suitable discipline, he is excluded from the church.

3. When a minister or any other member commits an offence in the vicinity of a church to which he does not belong, said church gives notice to the church of which he is a member, and the labor is commenced and ended in his own church.

4. When a trial exists in a church with a pastor or an ordained preacher, the church have the same right to discipline him as they have to discipline a private member. But in all cases of discipline with a minister, in which his Christian or ministerial character is likely to be affected, and when the trial is likely to result in his exclusion from the church, a council should be called to examine the case and give advice before the affair is finally concluded.

5. A minister who has been excluded for licentiousness should never be restored to the ministry again.

6. When a member declares his independence of the church and refuses to submit to gospel discipline, suit-

able efforts to reclaim him being unsuccessful, he should be excluded for disorderly walk.

7. In all difficult cases of discipline, a church has the right to call a council, or to apply to the Q. M. of which it is a member for a council, to assist them and give advice ; but no council or Q. M. can reverse the decisions of a church, or compel them against their wishes to retain a minister or a member in the church.

8. It is very desirable to have a unanimous vote in all the transactions of the church ; but when this cannot be obtained, the decisions, (except in the reception of members,) are made by a majority of the members present, and it is considered the duty of the minority to submit; or, if any considerable minority regard the doings of the majority as unscriptural, and the majority refuse to call a mutual council, the minority may present their trial with said church to the Q. M. of which the church is a member, and the Q. M. can take such action as they think advisable.

9. If a church neglect to exercise gospel discipline, offending members pass without admonition, and the complaints of the aggrieved are unheeded, those members who keep their covenant may commence discipline with the church for violating their covenant obligation. If their efforts prove unsuccessful, they can present to the Q. M. a request for assistance.

10. The minority of a church cannot consistently be approbated in withdrawing from the majority and forming a distinct organization, without the consent and co-operation of the Q. M. to which the church belongs.

11. When the majority of a church, connected with a Q. M. in regular standing in the denomination, comes to the conclusion to dissolve their connection with the Q. M., and consequently with the denomination, while at the same time a minority wish to adhere to their original organization, and to retain and maintain their standing as a Free-will Baptist church, it becomes the right and duty of such Q. M. to

recognize such minority by their request, as the original church.*

CHAPTER II.

QUARTERLY MEETINGS.

SECTION I. ORGANIZATION.

When two or more churches, not being situated within the limits of a Q. M., desire to associate in connection with the Free-will Baptist denomination, they may make application to a Quarterly or Yearly Meeting for a council, or they may select a council, to meet with delegates from these churches, to consult upon the expediency of organizing a Q. M. The council, on being assembled with the delegates, make a faithful examination in

* NOTE. During the time that an accusation against a member is entertained by the church, such member is suspended from the privileges of officiating as an officer, voting, or receiving the Lord's Supper.

regard to the order, sentiments, practice, fellowship and ability of these churches. If the examination prove satisfactory and the council are of the opinion that it will be for the interest of the cause of Christ to form these churches into a Q. M., they proceed to organize as follows:

1. A constitution for the government and regulation of the Q. M. is prepared, presented and adopted by the delegates in behalf of the churches which they represent.*

2. The delegates then arise and unite hands and agree in behalf of the churches to associate as a Q. M. for their mutual benefit, covenanting to govern themselves in all things agreeably to the Holy Scriptures.

3. One of the council then gives them the right hand of fellowship ac-

---

* This constitution should be prepared by a joint committee from all the churches which propose to unite in the Q. M., and be laid before the several churches and approved by them previous to the meeting for the organization of the Q. M.

knowledging them as a Q. M. properly constituted according to the usages of the Free-will Baptist denomination.

4. A consecrating prayer is then offered and a song of praise to the great Head of the Church.

5. The Q. M. then proceeds to the choice of the officers which are specified in the Constitution—the chairman of the council presiding till the officers are chosen.

6. By a vote of the Q. M. the clerk is instructed to prepare a written request for admission to membership into some Yearly Meeting in the Free-will Baptist connexion, and delegates are chosen to present the epistle to the Y. M.*

SECTION II. BUSINESS OF THE Q. M.

1. At each session, after the meet-

---

* NOTE. The constitution of a Q. M. contains the name of the Q. M., specifies the officers,—the time for holding its sessions and the number of delegates which each church should send to represent them in the Q. M.

ing is organized, the written reports and requests from the churches are received and read. New churches are received into membership when applications are made, and the examination is satisfactory.* Candidates for the ministry are examined for license and ordination when requests are made by the churches. Councils are appointed as occasion requires. Ministers are appointed occasionally, to visit and assist feeble churches. Resolutions on moral and religious subjects are frequently discussed and adopted.

2. At the session next preceding the session of the Y. M. to which the Q. M. belongs, delegates are chosen to attend the Y. M., and a letter, containing the statistics of the Q. M. written by the clerk, is forwarded by the delegates to the Y. M. [See form of report

---

* It is contrary to the usages of our denomination for a Q. M. to receive a church which has been excluded from another Q. M. for heresy or disorderly walk, unless that church first give satisfaction to the Q. M. from which it was excluded.

to Y. M. chap. VI. Sec. VI. Art. 3.]

3. The Q. M. sessions, which are held once in three months, usually continue three days. The business is generally transacted on the first day in the Q. M. conference, which is composed of the delegates from the churches. The Conferences usually sit with open doors, and any brother has the privilege to take part in the discussions; none, however, vote except the delegates. The last two days are generally devoted to public worship.

4. When a church in good standing requests a dismission to unite with another Q. M., or with another evangelical denomination, a letter of dismission and recommendation is given. Also, when a number of churches in good standing wish to be organized into a new Q. M., they are dismissed as above.

But it is contrary to the usages of the denomination for any church to dissolve its connection with the Q. M. without the consent of said Q. M.

SECTION III. DISCIPLINE OF THE Q. M.

1. A Q. M. cannot deprive a church of its independent form of government nor its right to discipline its own members, nor labor with individual members of churches as such; but, as the church is a member of the Q. M., it has the right to labor with the church as a body, in case of unscriptural or disorderly walk, and may determine whether the church is worthy of its fellowship or not.

2. When a church neglects to report itself to the Q. M. for two or three terms in succession, the Q. M. inquires into the cause of the neglect, and if satisfactory reasons are not given, the church is admonished.

3. When a church violates its covenant, becomes heretical, or corrupt in practice, the Q. M., on being apprised of the fact, investigates the matter, and after suitable labor, if unsuccessful, withdraws fellowship.

4. When a respectable minority of a Q. M. are grieved with the proceed-

ings of the majority, it is their privilege to present the cause of their grief to the Y. M. of which the Q. M. is a member, for redress.

CHAPTER III.

YEARLY MEETINGS.

SECTION I. ORGANIZATION.

A Yearly Meeting is composed of two or more Quarterly Meetings, associated in the same manner as the churches are in the formation of Q. Ms.

The method of organizing a Yearly Meeting is similar to that of a Quarterly Meeting. A council is called by the Quarterly Meetings which desire to unite in a Yearly Meeting. Delegates are chosen by the Q. Ms. to convene with the council. The council make a faithful examination in relation to the organization, condition, sentiments, order, and fellowship of the Q.

M. A constitution which has previously been approved by each Q. M. is read and adopted by the delegates present on behalf of their respective Q. Ms. One of the council gives the hand of fellowship to the delegates, thereby acknowledging the Q. Ms. which they represent, to be duly organized into a Y. M. A consecrating prayer and a song of praise then follow.

2. The chairman of the council presiding, the conference then proceed to the choice of the officers specified in the constitution.

3. By a vote of the Y. M. the clerk is instructed to prepare a written request to the General Conference for admission into that body, which is forwarded by the delegates of that Y. M. to the next session of the General Conference.

SECTION II. BUSINESS OF THE YEARLY MEETING.

1. At each session of the Yearly Meeting, letters containing reports of

the state of religion and the statistics of the Q. Ms. are received and read; also, requests from the Q. Ms. for advice, &c., are received and acted upon; councils and committees are appointed to assist in adjusting trials in Q. Ms. when necessary. New Q. Ms. are received when application is made and examination is satisfactory. Resolutions on moral and religious subjects are discussed, and such general measures adopted for the advancement of the benevolent enterprises, the spread of the gospel, and the promotion of order and holiness among the churches, as appear to be expedient.

2. At each session next preceding a session of the General Conference, delegates are chosen to represent the Y. M. in said conference. At this session also, the clerk prepares a letter to the General Conference. [See form of letter to the General Conference, Chap. VI. Sec. VII.]

3. The sessions of the Yearly Meeting usually continue three days, and are conducted in a manner similar to

Q. Ms. The Conference for business is composed of delegates from the Q. Ms. [See Ch. II. Sec. II. Art. 3.]

4. When a Q. M. in good standing requests a letter to join another Y. M., a letter of dismission is given. But it is contrary to the usages of the denomination for a Q. M. to dissolve its connection with the Y. M. without the consent of said Y. M.

SECTION III. DISCIPLINE OF THE Y. M.

1. Every Y. M. has the same right to discipline the Q. Ms. of which it is composed, as a Q. M. has to discipline the churches which belong to it, and for the same reasons. The Y. M. cannot reverse the decisions of a Q. M. nor labor with individual churches, but it can labor with the Q. M. as a body in case the Q. M. pursues an unscriptural or disorderly course.

2. When a Q. M. neglects to report itself, or when it becomes heretical, or corrupt in practice, the Y. M. pursues the same course with it that a Q. M. does with a disorderly church.

3. When a respectable minority of a Y. M. are grieved with the majority, it is their privilege to present their complaint to the General Conference, with a request for assistance.

CHAPTER IV.

GENERAL CONFERENCE.

SECTION I. DESIGN OF THE GENERAL CONFERENCE.

1. The General Conference is designed to comprise all the Yearly Meetings in the Free-will Baptist denomination in North America, and to complete the organization of the connexion—to consolidate the body by harmonizing its different parts, keeping a common interest in view, and producing unity of sentiment and discipline—to concentrate its strength in the common cause of the Redeemer, and by a fraternal interchange of views

among its members, to promote a growth in grace, and a knowledge of gospel truth.

2. The General Conference sustains the same relation to the Y. Ms. as Y. Ms. do to the Q. Ms., or Q. Ms. to the churches of which they are composed.

3. This body was organized in 1827. In 1841, it adopted the following Constitution and By-Laws, by which it is governed.

Section II. Constitution and By-Laws of the General Conference.

Article 1. This Conference shall be called the General Conference of the Free-will Baptist Connexion in North America; and shall be composed of delegates chosen from Yearly Meetings of said connexion, which Yearly Meetings shall have been recognized as such by the Conference in the manner mentioned in the 2d article of this Constitution.

Art. 2. Any Yearly Meeting may

be received as a body into this Conference by vote of three-fourths of the members present at any regular session. It shall be the duty of Yearly Meetings themselves to report by delegation and letter to each session of Conference, giving in their letters their statistics.

Art. 3. Each Yearly Meeting belonging to this Conference shall be entitled to representation by one delegate; and every Yearly Meeting, whose church communicants amount to one thousand five hundred, to two delegates, and one additional delegate to each additional thousand church members.

Art. 4. The stated sessions of this Conference shall be held once in two years, to commence on the 1st Wednesday in Oct. at 10 o'clock, A. M., the place for each session to be designated by the session next preceding, or by a committee appointed by such preceding session for that purpose. Extra sessions may be appointed, or the time between sessions lengthened, by a vote of two thirds of the members present at any session of Conference.

Art. 5. The officers of this Conference shall consist of a standing clerk, who shall retain his office until he resigns or another be chosen to fill his place—a moderator, assistant moderator, and assistant clerks, to be chosen at each session. Said officers to be chosen by ballot, or by nomination of a committee appointed for that purpose.

Art. 6. It shall be the duty of the standing clerk to keep a record of the doings of the Conference. It shall be the duty of the moderator to preside in the sessions of the Conference. It shall be the duty of the assistant officers to perform the duties usually devolving upon such officers.

Art. 7. It shall be the duty of the Conference to receive and act upon communications from the Yearly Meetings properly belonging to this body—to exercise supervision over the Printing establishment, and to consult for the interests of religion in the Free-will Baptist denomination.

Art. 8. The Conference shall have the right to discipline, and, if necessary, exclude such Yearly Meetings and other associations as may be connected with it; but in no case shall it have power to reverse or change the decisions of churches, Quarterly or Yearly Meetings, or any other religious bodies.

Art. 9. This Conference may make such By-Laws and Regulations, not repugnant to this Constitution, as it may deem necessary.

Art. 10. This Constitution may be amended at any regular session of this Conference by vote of two thirds of the members present, provided such amendment has been proposed at a previous session, published in the Minutes of that session, and approved by at least three-fourths of the Y. Ms. belonging to the Conference.

[The above instrument having been accepted by three-fourths of the Yearly Meetings, was acknowledged as the

Constitution of the General Conference of the Free-will Baptist connexion at the eleventh session of that body, held in 1841.]

BY-LAWS.

Art. 1. Each session of this Conference shall be called to order by the standing clerk when present, and in his absence by the member having seniority of years.

Art. 2. Each session and adjourned sitting of the Conference shall be opened and closed by prayer.

Art. 3. Twenty members shall be required to constitute a quorum to transact any business of this Conference. But any less number may adjourn from time to time.

Art. 4. After the opening of each session of this Conference, a chairman shall be appointed, and a committee of not less than three persons shall be chosen to examine credentials for membership in the Conference. After the report of this committee and enrollment of members present, the Conference shall proceed to the election of moderator and to the transaction of other business.

Art. 5. At each session of this Conference, standing committees shall be appointed on such subjects as the following: Printing Establishment--Education--Sabbath Schools --Temperance--Ministry--Slavery--Missions --Correspondence--Moral Reform--and Popery. All petitions and communications on particular subjects shall be referred to their appropriate committees. Special committees may be appointed at the pleasure of the Conference.

Art. 6. This Conference may hold correspondence by messenger or otherwise with other religious bodies as it may deem advisable.

Art. 7. This Conference shall sit with open doors except when it may go into committee of the whole.

Art. 8. Any person not a member of this Conference may be allowed to take part in its discussions by obtaining permission of the Conference.

Art. 9. It shall be the duty of the standing clerk to furnish each session of the Conference with a book of records containing the doings of its previous sessions.

Art. 10. The Conference may commence and close its sessions at the time it shall determine at each session.

Art. 11. It shall be the duty of all the members of this Conference to be present at the time appointed for each sitting, and any one wishing to retire while Conference is in sitting shall first obtain leave of the moderator.

Art. 12. No member shall absent himself from Conference during its sessions without first obtaining permission from the Conference.

Art. 13. Every member wishing to speak

in Conference shall first address the moderator.

Art. 14. No person shall be allowed to speak more than ten minutes at any one time, nor more than twice on any subject, without leave of Conference.

Art. 15. No debate shall be allowed on any motion except the same be submitted in writing and seconded by a member of Conference.

Art. 16. No whispering shall be allowed during the sittings of Conference without leave of the moderator; but all the members shall pay strict attention to the business of Conference.

Art. 17. No person shall be allowed to nominate more than one member on any committee whatever, provided the brother nominated be elected.

Art. 18. The yeas and nays may be taken on any question before the Conference by request of one fifth of the members present.

Art. 19. The Constitution and By-Laws of this Conference shall be read at each session near its commencement.

CHAPTER V.

MINISTERS' CONFERENCES.

These conferences are composed of ministers in the same Quarterly or

Yearly Meeting who associate for mutual benefit, and the interests of Zion. Their meetings are held occasionally as circumstances require.

1. The subjects which are generally discussed in these Conferences, are as follows:

(1) The best methods for promoting the interests of pure religion.

(2) The evils which exist among us, and the manner in which they should be removed.

(3) The unity of the ministry in doctrine and discipline.

(4) The state of Christian fellowship in the ministry.

(5) The manner and the places in which the ministry may best employ their time and devote their services.

(6) The meaning of certain passages of Scripture.

2. The members of these Conferences consider themselves under each other's particular care, and that it is their duty to watch over, admonish, rebuke, and exhort one another with all long suffering and diligence.

3. If at any time a Conference ascertains a case of immoral conduct, or heresy of sentiment in any one of its members, it reports the same to the church of which he is a member.

4. These Conferences are usually governed by such Constitution and By-Laws as the members are disposed to adopt, not repugnant to the general polity of the Free-will Baptist denomination.

CHAPTER VI.

FORMS.

SECTION I. CONFESSION OF FAITH* AND CHURCH COVENANT.

ARTICLE 1. *Inspiration of the Scriptures.* We believe that the Scriptures of the Old and New Testaments are given by inspiration of God.

---

* This confession of faith contains a summary of the doctrines of F. W. Baptists. Every church is of course at liberty to adopt the whole, or such parts of it as they think best.

Art. 2. *One God.* We believe that there is one only living and true God, the self-existent author of all beings, infinite in all his attributes.

Art. 3. *One Savior.* We believe that there is one mediator between God and man, the Lord Jesus Christ, who, in his character as a Savior, possessed a human nature which was truly man, and a divine nature which was truly God.

Art. 4. *The Holy Spirit.* We believe in the personality of the Holy Spirit, the reprover of the world, and the Comforter of the saints, who possesses all the attributes of God.

Art. 5. *The Trinity.* We believe that the Father, Son and Holy Spirit, are one God; the same in essence, power and glory.

Art. 6. *Purposes and Providences of God.* We believe the purposes of God are eternal and immutable; that He created all things for his own glory; and that his providence and government are universal, wise, and holy.

Art. 7. *Man's Original State and*

Fall. We believe that man was created pure and upright; but, by their own transgression, our first parents fell from their original state of rectitude into a state of condemnation, and in consequence of their fall, their posterity inherit propensities to evil—possess a carnal mind, which is enmity against God; and that those propensities are strengthened by indulgence; and none who come to years of discretion can enjoy God's favor or truly love God without regeneration, or a new heart, which is produced by Divine agency.

Art. 8. *The Atonement.* We believe that Christ by his sufferings and death has made an atonement for every individual of the human family without distinction of persons, which atonement is as full and as free for every one as for any one, and that through this atonement is the only way of salvation.

Art. 9. *Salvation by Grace.* We believe that no man can come unto Christ except the Father draw him by his Spirit, and that no man can come unto the Father but by Christ; that the gift of the Holy Spirit and the atonement of Christ are entirely of grace—therefore, by grace are we saved.

Art. 10. *Election.* We believe that God has not fixed the future state of mankind by any unconditional decree, but determined from all eternity to save those whom he foresaw would comply with the conditions of salvation; and that this is the only election to salvation which is taught in the Bible.

Art. 11. *Salvation practicable.* We believe that God wills the salvation of all men, that the gospel invites all, that the Holy Spirit enables all to accept salvation, and that whosoever will may take the water of life freely.

Art. 12. *Freedom of the Will.* We believe that the will of man is free, irresistibly controlled by no other power, it being a self-controlling power—that by the exercise of this faculty, man yields to the motives which God places before him, seeks regenerating grace, and secures eternal life, or rejects these motives and perishes.

Art. 13. *Conditions of Salvation.* We believe that repentance and active faith in Jesus Christ and his atonement must be exercised by all those who have committed actual sins, in order to secure to them the benefits of that atonement, the regenerating influence of God's grace, and eternal life.

Art. 14. *Perseverance.* We believe that only such believers as persevere in a life of holiness unto the end, will be eternally saved.

Art. 15. *The Sabbath.* We believe that the Christian Sabbath is a divine institution, and should be observed by abstaining from all sinful amusements and secular business, and devoted to the worship of God.

Art. 16. *Ordinances of the gospel.* We believe that baptism or the immersion of believers in water, and the sacrament of the Lord's supper, are ordinances to be perpetuated in the church and administered to all true believers.

Art. 17. *The Resurrection and Judg-*

ment. We believe in the second coming of Christ to judge the world, when the dead will be raised, and the righteous received into eternal felicity, and the wicked banished eternally from the presence of God, into everlasting suffering.

COVENANT.

Sincerely believing that it is the duty of all who love our God and Savior to unite with the visible church of Christ, and believing that we have earnestly sought and obtained the regenerating influences of divine grace through Jesus Christ, and having renounced the world and the things of the world, and having been buried with Christ in baptism, and having adopted the foregoing as our Confession of Faith,

We do now solemnly covenant before God, that we will strive by his assisting grace to exemplify our confession by a practice which shall correspond to all which we have above professed. And we do now give ourselves publicly and renewedly to God, to love and serve him till death—and to his people, to live together with them in brotherly love and union. And we do solemnly covenant that we will exercise a mutual Christian care and watchfulness over each other, and will faithfully labor for the promotion of each other's spiritual welfare by fervent prayer, faithful admonitions, and affectionate rebukes, if necessary—will endeavor to restore the erring in the spirit of meekness, and labor together by prayer, precept, and example, for the salvation of sinners.

We do covenant that we will contribute of our substance for the support of a faithful ministry among us, and for all other necessary means of grace, and will be benevolent to the needy, and especially to the poor of our own church, and we will, as far as we are able, attend upon the public worship of God and the stated meetings of the church, and will labor for its prosperity and upbuilding in the most holy faith; and will not forsake it in adversity, but will bear each other's burdens and so fulfil the law of Christ. We will constantly maintain secret and family devotion, and religiously instruct those under our care, and will cordially cooperate with those who minister to us in holy things, and will esteem them highly in love for their work's sake.

We covenant that we will not traffic in, nor use intoxicating drinks, as a beverage, and that we will sustain the other benevolent enterprises of the day, as Missions, Sabbath Schools, Moral Reform, Anti-Slavery, Education, and all others which, in the use of holy means, tend to the glory of God and the welfare of man.

We covenant and agree that we will love all those who love our Lord Jesus Christ; that we will avoid all vain extravagance and sinful conformity to the world, and will abstain from all sinful amusements, as theatres, dances, gambling, and from all vain festivals; and will refrain from all unchaste and profane conversation, and from the reading of wicked and corrupting publications. We will walk circumspectly towards those who are without, that the cause of God may not be reproached on our acconnt.

And may the God of peace sanctify us wholly, and preserve us blameless to the coming of our Lord Jesus Christ, to join the glorified around the throne of God, in ascribing blessing, and honor, and glory and power, unto him that sitteth on the throne, and unto the Lamb forever and ever. Amen.

SECTION II. LETTER OF DISMISSION

M—— N. H.—— 185—,

THIS CERTIFIES THAT —— —— is a regular member of the ——— FREE-WILL BAPTIST CHURCH in —— ——— in good standing, and as such, we commend —— to the fellowship of God's people; and when we are informed that —— has united with some other evangelical church, we shall consider — regularly dismissed from this church.

In behalf of the Free will Baptist church in ————.

—— ——, PASTOR.

—— ——, *Clerk.*

SECTION III. CERTIFICATE OF LICENSE.

THIS CERTIFIES that the bearer, —— ——, of the town of ———————, county of ———— State of ————————, being a member in good standing of the —— Free-will Baptist church in said ————, has this day received license to preach the gospel for one year, and is hereby commended to the fellowship of the saints.

In behalf of the Q. M.

(Signed) —— ——, *Clerk.*

(Date)

SECTION IV. CERTIFICATE OF ORDINATION.

This certifies that the bearer, ———————, of the town of ———— county of ————————, State of ————————, a regular member of the —— Free-will Baptist church in said ————, has this day been publicly set apart to the work of the ministry, by prayer and the imposition of hands, according to the usage of the Free-will

Baptist denomination, and is hereby authorized to preach the gospel and administer its ordinances, wherever God in his providence may call him.

(Signed) ——— ———, ——— ———, ——— ———, } *Ordaining Council.*

(Date)

SECTION V. EPISTLE FROM A CHURCH TO A Q. M.

A report from a church to a Q. M. among other things usually embraces the following:—

1. An account of the state of religion.

2. The state of union in the church.

3. The degree of interest in public and social meetings.

4. The condition of the Sabbath school and the interest manifested in missions, and other benevolent enterprises.

5. Any request or petition from a church for a council, the examination of a minister, or for the next Q. M., &c.

6. Names of delegates.

The letter to the next session of the Q. M. after the first Sabbath in April should contain the statistics of the church, as follows :—

1. The number of members added by baptism during the preceding year, ending on the first Sabbath in April. 2. The number added by letter during the same time. 3. The number dismissed. 4. The number excluded. 5. The number died. 6. The present number in good standing. 7. The names of the ministers who are members of the church, and whether they are licensed or ordained.

SECTION VI. EPISTLE FROM A Q. M. TO A Y. M.

A letter from a Q. M. to a Y. M. usually embraces the following particulars.

1. The general state of religion and accounts of revivals if any have occurred during the preceding year.

2. The state of the Sabbath schools in the churches of the Q. M. and the interest manifested in the great moral questions.

3. Statistics of the Q. M. in the following form :*

Names of Churches.	Added by Baptism.	Added by Letter.	Dismissed.	Excluded.	Died.	Present number.	Ministers Ordained.	Ministers Licensed.	No. of Elders.	No. of Licentiates.	Net increase or decrease.
Boston,	25	20	13	3	2	150	1	2	2	2	
Lowell,	40	17	20	1	24	422		1	1	1	
Roxbury,	30	12	5		3	142			1	1	
Lawr'nce	23	19		3		60			1		
Total, 4	118	69	38	7	29	774	1	3	5	4	100

4. The number of churches which have been added to the Q. M. during the preceding year, and the number which have been dismissed and excluded from it.

5. Names of the delegates to the Y. M.

6. Questions, petitions and requests.

---

* It is desirable that the annual statistics of the entire denomination should be made to the same date, that they may correspond. We would therefore earnestly recommend that all statistical returns from year to year, for Q. Ms. and the Register, be computed to the second week in April.

Committee of Revision.

SECTION VII. EPISTLE FROM A Y. M. TO THE GENERAL CONFERENCE.

1. This epistle takes up in similar order the same topics which are embraced in the epistles to the smaller bodies, treating upon the changes which have taken place in the Y. M. since the preceding session of the General Conference, the statistics, embracing the alterations of the three years which have intervened between the second week in April of the year in which the preceding Conference was held, and the same date in the year in which the returns are made, in the following form:

	Added by Baptism.	Added by Letter.	Dismissed.	Excluded.	Died.	Churches Added.	Churches Dismissed.	Churches Excluded.	Ministers Ordained.	Ministers Licensed.	Net increase or decrease of memb'rs.
1848	120	80	67	20	2	3	1	2	4	5	
1849	240	100	47	60	10	11		1	10	14	
1850	360	120	50	20	14	16	2		15	20	
	720	300	104	100	26	30	3	3	29	39	

2. To this report is added the number and names of the Q. Ms., the whole number of churches, members, Elders and Licentiates in the Y. M. at the date of the last returns. If any Q. Ms. have been added, dismissed or excluded, or lost their visibility, such fact is included in the report.

3. Names of delegates to the General Conference.

SECTION VIII. QUARTERLY MEETING CONSTITUTION.

Article 1. This Quarterly Meeting shall be called the
and shall be composed of such consistent, well regulated Free-will Baptist churches as shall unite in this compact, and agree to this constitution.

2. The acting members of the Conference of this Q. M. shall be such as are chosen by the several churches of which the Q. M. is composed to represent them in Q. M. Conference, every church being entitled to one delegate, every church containing fifty members to two delegates, and one additional

delegate for every additional twenty-five members.

3. The officers of this Q. M. shall be a Moderator, who shall be chosen at every quarterly session, and a Clerk and a Treasurer, who shall be standing officers of the Q. M., all of whom shall be expected to discharge such duties as usually devolve on such officers.

4. Any regularly organized Free-will Baptist church, maintaining gospel order, agreeing with the denomination in doctrines and practice, and in favor of the benevolent enterprises, as Sabbath Schools, Missions, Temperance, Abolition of Slavery, Education, &c., may be received into this Q. M. on application by a vote of the Conference to which such application is made or referred.

5. This Q. M. shall have power to discipline its churches for unchristian conduct, a want of conformity to gospel order, or a violation of the conditions of this compact, and expel them in case of unsuccessful labor; to license and ordain as ministers such as give

evidence of being qualified and called of God, by request of churches to which such persons belong,—to settle such questions of discipline and doctrine as the churches may refer to them, and transact such other business as may be necessary for the benefit of the cause of God, consistent with the liberty and independence of the churches—accordant with the usages of the Free-will Baptist denomination, and not repugnant to the regulations of the Yearly Meeting with which this Q. M. may be connected, and to make any by-laws necessary to its regulation, not repugnant to this constitution.

6. The sessions of this Q. M. shall be on the ,
when it shall be the duty of all the churches of which it is composed to represent themselves by letter and by delegates.

7. This Constitution may be altered or amended by a vote of any session of the Q. M., notice of such intended alteration having been given at a previous session of the conference.

SECTION IX. YEARLY MEETING CONSTITUTION.

1. This Yearly Meeting shall be called the
and shall be composed of such regularly organized and well disciplined Free-will Baptist Quarterly Meetings, conveniently located, as may embody themselves under this constitution.

2. The Conference of this Yearly Meeting shall consist of delegates from the several Quarterly Meetings of which it is composed, every Q. M. being entitled to one delegate, every Q. M. containing five hundred members to two delegates, and one additional delegate for every additional five hundred members.

3. The officers of this Y. M. shall be a standing Clerk and Treasurer;—and a Moderator, to be chosen at every session of the Y. M., with such assistants as may be found necessary.

4. Any consistent, well organized and well regulated Free-will Baptist Quarterly Meeting, composed of such churches as conform to the usages and

adopt the doctrines of the Free-will Baptist denomination, as published in the Treatise on their Faith and in the minutes of the sessions of the General Conference, and is in favor of all the benevolent enterprises in which the denomination are engaged, may at any time, on application, by a vote of this Y. M. become a member thereof.

5. This Yearly Meeting shall have power to discipline the Quarterly Meetings of which it is composed, and to exclude them for disorderly walk, if labor proves unsuccessful; but in no case to reverse their decisions nor interfere with any of their internal regulations.

6. The sessions of this Yearly Meeting shall be held on , at which time it shall be the duty of the Quarterly Meetings of which the Y. M. is composed to represent themselves by delegates, and report their standing and prospects and statistics by letter: and at which time the Yearly Meeting shall act upon such questions and topics as may be refer-

red to them by their respective Quarterly Meetings, and transact such other business, not repugnant to this constitution nor to the usages of the denomination, as in their judgment may forward the cause of Christ and the interests of the churches and Q. Ms. within the limits of the Y. M.

7. This Y. M. shall have power to adopt any regulations or by-laws, not inconsistent with this Constitution, which may be deemed essential to the farther regulation of its sessions.

8. This Constitution may be altered or amended by a vote of the Y. M. at any session, notice of such intended alteration having been duly given and recorded at any previous session.

INDEX.

USAGES OF THE F. W. BAPTIST CONNEXION.

www.ingramcontent.com/pod-product-compliance
Lightning Source LLC
LaVergne TN
LVHW011233110826
845150LV00006B/1623

9781425514365